Pittsburgh's
CIVIC ARENA

Pittsburgh's CIVIC ARENA

STORIES FROM THE IGLOO

THE ASSOCIATION OF GENTLEMAN PITTSBURGH JOURNALISTS

THE
History
PRESS

Published by The History Press
Charleston, SC
www.historypress.com

Front cover, top left: courtesy of David Finoli; *top center*: courtesy of Duquesne University Athletics; *top right*: courtesy of the University of Pittsburgh Athletics; *bottom*: courtesy of David Finoli.
Back cover: courtesy of Duquesne University Athletics.

Opposite: Norm Nixon is one of the iconic figures in Duquesne basketball history, leading them to their last NCAA tournament to date in 1977 and was the Eastern Eight Player of the Year that season. The school eventually retired his number in 2001. He went on to score 12,065 points in his NBA career, which included two NBA titles with the Los Angeles Lakers. *Courtesy of Duquesne Athletics.*

First published 2021

Manufactured in the United States

ISBN 9781467148849

Library of Congress Control Number: 2021943436

To our fathers, our families, our friends and our children. The memories we shared with them at the Civic Arena is what makes this facility so special to us.

CONTENTS

ACKNOWLEDGEMENTS   13

INTRODUCTION   15

PART I. THE STRUCTURE

1. Finding the Duquesne Gardens, by David Finoli   18
2. That Amazing Roof That Opens, by Jack Mathison   21
3. Why the Civic Arena Became the Mellon Arena…and Not
    the Mellon Financial Center, by Tom Rooney   26
4. Tear the Roof Off the Sucker: Creating a Collectible Ornament
    Forged from the Civic Arena Roof, by Chris Fletcher   29
5. The Civic Arena Dome Still Shines in Cory Bonnet's Art,
    by Tom Rooney   33

PART II. HOCKEY

6. 1967 Penguins (Try to) Take Flight in Pittsburgh,
    by Tom Rooney   38
7. The Definition of Balanced Scoring: The 1974–75 Penguins,
    by Paul Alexander   42
8. Lucky Pierre: The Penguins' First Gate Attraction,
    by John Wdowiak   46
9. Tanks for the Memories: The 1983–84 Penguins' Quest
    to Finish Last, by Chris Fletcher   50
10. Lord Stanley, Lord Stanley, Give Me the Brandy:
    The Championship Era Begins, by John Wdowiak   54

11. Dynasty Unfulfilled, by Paul Alexander ... 59
12. The Lemieux Hat Trick, by Paul Alexander ... 63
13. Saying Goodbye: The Pens' Final Season at the Igloo,
by John W. Franko ... 67
14. Going Out on Top: The Hornets Say Goodbye with a Calder Cup,
by John W. Franko ... 72
15. The Summit at Center Ice: The Russians Come to Pittsburgh,
by Gary Kinn ... 76

PART III. MUSIC
16. The Boss: Bruce Springsteen Makes His Impact on the Civic Arena,
by Lance Jones ... 82
17. The Fabs and the King: Rock's Highest Royalty Graced the Arena
with Their Presence—If I Had Only Been There,
by Chris Fletcher ... 87
18. The Skyline Series, by Lance Jones ... 91
19. The Troubadours: An Appropriate Way to Close the Curtain
on the Civic Arena, by Rich Boyer ... 95

PART IV. BASKETBALL
20. The Day the NBA Died in Pittsburgh, by David Finoli ... 100
21. When Adversity Meets Opportunity: The Pittsburgh Rens,
by Gary Kinn ... 104
22. The Hawk Makes His Mark on the 'Burgh: The Story of the
Pittsburgh Pipers, by Josh Taylor ... 107
23. The Sad, Strange Tale of the Pittsburgh Condors,
by Frank Garland ... 111
24. The Dapper Dan Roundball Classic: High School Basketball
Takes Center Stage, by Frank Garland ... 116
25. The Eastern Eight Tournament: Before It All Busted Up,
by Josh Taylor ... 121
26. The City Game, by John W. Franko ... 126
27. Dave and Chris's Excellent Adventure: The 1997 NCAA
Basketball Tournament, by David Finoli ... 131
28. A Panther Homecoming: The 2002 NCAA Basketball
Tournament, by Josh Taylor ... 135

Contents

PART V. WRESTLING AND BOXING

29. Remembering *Studio Wrestling* and "The Living Legend"
Bruno Sammartino, by Robert Healy III 140
30. Hell in an Igloo: Mick Foley Shocks, Amazes Pittsburgh Crowd,
by Robert Healy III 144
31. Gaseous Cassius Invades the Smoky City,
by Douglas Cavanaugh 148
32. "Golden" Glory: Amateur Boxing at Pittsburgh's Civic Arena
Created Lasting Memories, by Robert Healy III 152
*Addendum: High School Classic Brought Amateur Wrestling Greatness
to Civic Arena* 155
33. Even the Best Laid Plans: Holmes Versus Snipes,
by Gary Kinn 157
34. A Closed-Circuit Love Affair, by David Finoli 161

PART VI. OTHER TEAMS AND EVENTS

35. A War on the Floor: The Civic Arena Welcomes...Arena Football!,
by Tom Rooney 166
36. In the Spirit: My Oh-So-Brief Affair with Indoor Soccer,
by Chris Fletcher 170
37. The Triangles: Pittsburgh's Last Title Won Under the Igloo Roof,
by David Finoli 173
38. Elephants, Dogs and Rats, Oh My!: Animals at the Civic Arena,
by Jack Mathison 177
39. Forgotten but...Well...Still Forgotten: The Other Teams and
Events at the Igloo We May Not Remember,
by David Finoli 179

BIBLIOGRAPHY 183
ABOUT THE AUTHORS 185

There were few if any more honored basketball players in Duquesne University history than **B.B.** Flenory (15). A first-team All–Eastern Eight player in 1980, when he led the league with 20.4 points per game, Flenory finished his Duke career with 1,382 points, becoming the only player in the program's history to lead the team in scoring and assists for three consecutive seasons. *Courtesy of Duquesne Athletics.*

ACKNOWLEDGEMENTS

Creating a book is certainly an effort that brings the passion of the subject out in the people who tell the story. This one was no different for the fourteen authors who tell the story of one of the most iconic sports facilities that has ever been built in the city of Pittsburgh, the Civic Arena. As much effort as it took from us to put this book together, its completion could not have been done without the help of others.

With the time we put in over and above our normal workdays, a thank-you goes out to our families and friends for the support they gave us throughout the process. This couldn't have been achieved without them.

There was also talented Pittsburgh artist Cory Bonnet, who donated his time for chapter 5 and three of his incredible works to the project. There is also the Riskus family, Ida D'Ericco, Steve Easton of the University of Toledo, Brian Deutsch of the University of Minnesota, Alastair Ingram of Boston College, Duquesne University's David Saba, Matt Plizga and E.J. Borghetti of the University of Pittsburgh and, finally, Amanda Aikens, the sister of the late Tom Aikens. She generously allowed us to use the photos in the book. Her photo donations are very much appreciated.

We also would like to thank Pierre LaRouche, Rich Engler, Ed Traversari and Joe Grushecky, along with many others who helped us with the various chapters of this book.

Finally, we'd like to thank The History Press, especially our editor Rick Delaney and Banks Smither, who has been an incredible partner for all of the books the Association of Gentleman Pittsburgh Journalists has written. Without the help of all, this book would not have been a possibility.

—DF

INTRODUCTION

The majority of the authors in this book are proud graduates of Duquesne University. We all have the same shared memories of seeing the Civic Arena (or the Mellon Arena, depending on when we attended the school) from the campus. In the pre–Palumbo Center days, it's where our Dukes played their home games. But there were so many more reasons we'd travel the few blocks from the Bluff (the part of town where Duquesne was located) to the front doors of this memorable facility.

For all of us, it was the only indoor major-league arena we knew. I had the pleasure of seeing a Triangle match, as well as a Monkees concert, with the facility's famed retractable roof open. I attended a Gladiator game in which one of our contributors, Tom Rooney, took hell from the coach for instructing the powers that be to open the roof during the game.

It's where we, to a man, fell in love with the Penguins. For the older authors in these pages, we suffered for years buying five-dollar tickets in the upper deck, only to find ourselves on the glass by the end of the first period because the crowds were small. Every so often the franchise showed glimpses of success, but inevitably they'd break our hearts in ways that were not imaginable. They even tanked the end of a season to see just how bad they could be. It turned out to be arguably the greatest moment in franchise history. They tanked so badly that the team was able to draft a young player who, five decades later, still leads this team to greatness. That story is told here by Chris Fletcher, a man I suffered with through those times.

Unlike Three Rivers Stadium, the main purpose of the facility was not to house one or two franchises. There were others, such as the Spirit, the Pipers, the Condors, the Rens and the Stingers. Please don't forget the Stingers....I see you already have. There was also music, lots and lots of music. In fact, the concerts were almost as important as the sporting events. The greats of the industry—the Beatles, Elvis, James Taylor and, my personal favorite, Bruce Springsteen—played under the famed Igloo ceiling. Chris, Lance Jones and Rich Boyer bring those memories to life.

We had dates there. We brought our children. We spent many moments with our close friends, with each other and with our wives. The memories are thick and are told magnificently by not only the authors just mentioned but also Gary Kinn, Josh Taylor, John Franko, Frank Garland, Robert Healy III, Paul Alexander, John Wdowiak, Jack Mathison and, last but certainly not least, Douglas Cavanaugh.

It was an extreme honor to share the pages of this book with each and every one of them and to bring back those special events, moments, bands, teams and players that made the Arena so special. And now I present the Civic Arena, as we celebrate the sixtieth anniversary of its opening.

—David Finoli

PART I

THE STRUCTURE

1

FINDING THE DUQUESNE GARDENS

BY DAVID FINOLI

Before the city's sports facilities moved to the center of Pittsburgh and the North Side, the epicenter of sports in the Steel City was in the Oakland section, in the heart of the University of Pittsburgh. Forbes Field, Pitt Stadium and the Fitzgerald Field House were the well-known places that called Oakland home, but there was an arena that housed winning teams in an era—the 1940s and '50s—when the Pirates, Pitt football and the Steelers often struggled. It was called the Duquesne Gardens. Since I hadn't yet been born during the time when the Hornets and Duquesne basketball thrilled Pittsburgh sports fans there, I was determined to find where it stood. I wanted to try to let the memories of the championships won there sink in, to travel to 110 North Craig Street in Oakland, where it was razed in 1956 to make space for an apartment building and an iconic restaurant that no longer stands there either, Stouffer's. I was on a quest to find the place that housed Pittsburgh indoor sports before the Civic Arena was built: the Duquesne Gardens.

I begin my tour where I had so many times before, at the remnants of Forbes Field. A portion of the outfield wall was left intact after the historic ballpark was torn down. It was where the great college football teams of the beginning of the twentieth century were housed and was the Steelers' first home. It was also where its main tenant, the Pirates, toiled for sixty-one years. Forbes Field was where Honus Wagner, Paul Waner and Roberto

Clemente played and where Bill Mazeroski smacked the greatest home run in baseball history that set this city on fire in 1960.

I stroll up Roberto Clemente Drive to Schenley Drive and take a left on Forbes Avenue. I then see the Cathedral of Learning, one of the most iconic views in the city of Pittsburgh. Behind it and to the left is the Petersen Events Center, a state-of-the-art facility where the Panther basketball team now plays. It's on that site where Pitt Stadium once stood. I made the trip up Cardiac Hill many times to see some of the nationally ranked Pitt football teams play in the late 1970s and early '80s. It was there where not only the great Carnegie Tech teams played before World War II and the Steelers in the 1960s, but also where the Panthers were the dominant team in the nation under Jock Sutherland, winning five national championships. Across the street from "the Pete" is the Fitzgerald Field House, the establishment for Pitt's basketball team and, for a time, Duquesne University's basketball team. It still stands and is currently the home to, among other teams, the Panthers' nationally ranked wrestling and women's volleyball teams.

As I pass the famed Carnegie Museum of Natural History, I see South Craig Street. My quest is almost complete. I've spent an incredible amount of time in Oakland over the years, but for whatever reason I can't remember a time when I found myself walking on Craig Street as an adult.

There is a plethora of restaurants with great reputations as I stroll up South Craig: the Union Grill, Lucca and Little Asia, to name a few. I think about stopping at each to get a bite, but I resist. This journey is about seeing where the Gardens stood, not filling my stomach—although I guess it's no crime to do both. Anyway, the journey continues.

I reach Fifth Avenue where South Craig Street turns into North Craig Street. Only a few feet up is 110 North Craig, where the Duquesne Gardens stood. It's right across from St. Paul's Cathedral and is now a collection of apartment buildings. I've driven past St. Paul's many times and even attended Mass there on occasion. I've seen those apartment buildings but never put it together that this is where the historic venue stood.

In my mind I can only imagine a bustling corner where many Steel City sports fans got their fix. Built in 1890 as a streetcar barn for the Duquesne Traction Company, the facility was remodeled six years later, and the Duquesne Gardens was born. At the beginning of the twentieth century, it was lauded as the world's largest ice-skating arena, where it also played host to a theater and an indoor sporting arena.

It eventually became home to many college, amateur and professional teams, including the city's first National Hockey League franchise, the Pittsburgh Pirates, and the Pittsburgh Ironmen of the Basketball Association of America, a precursor to the National Basketball Association. But the two most famous franchises to call it home were the city's longtime American Hockey League franchise, the Hornets, and Duquesne University basketball.

It was there in 1955 that Pittsburgh's reputation as the "City of Champions" first took root, when the Hornets captured their second Calder Cup title and the Dukes won their lone national championship with a win in the then-prestigious National Invitation Tournament. A year later, the facility was gone, torn down to make space for apartments and Stouffer's.

It was five years before the city had a suitable place for professional hockey, when the Civic Arena opened. The Hornets, who had been dormant for five seasons, finally resurfaced at that point, and Duquesne basketball soon followed to play there, much closer to campus.

Today, many sports fans don't know of the existence of the Duquesne Gardens. Make no mistake, it was an extremely important part of the city's history. I now gaze upon the grounds where Baz Bastien, Chuck Cooper, Dick Ricketts and Sihugo Green became Pittsburgh legends. My journey is now complete, and I have a sense where Pittsburgh sports took shape before the Igloo was even a glint in the eyes of Steel City sports fans.

2

THAT AMAZING ROOF THAT OPENS

BY JACK MATHISON

The shiny dome on the hill that was the Civic Arena began as an idea of Edgar J. Kaufmann, a department store magnate, to find a suitable home for the Civic Light Opera. The CLO, of which Kaufmann was president, held summer operatic performances at Pitt Stadium. Kaufmann felt it needed a suitable home that was truly unique. He began to pitch his idea to the City of Pittsburgh and Allegheny County officials as early as 1948. The Public Auditorium Authority of Pittsburgh and Allegheny County was formed in 1954 to fund and operate the Civic Auditorium Amphitheater, the original name of the facility.

Construction began on March 12, 1958, and concluded with the official opening on September 17, 1961. The $22 million venue was the first major entertainment and sports facility in the world with a retractable roof. The structure covered 170,000 square feet with a diameter of 415 feet and held over three thousand tons of Pittsburgh steel. The roof was composed of eight separate leaves. The roof was supported by a huge cantilevered steel arm on the east side that was 260 feet long and approximately 130 feet high at its peak over the center of the main floor. The six movable leaves separated on the west (downtown) side of the building, and each leaf retracted over the adjacent leaf back to nest over the two stationary fixed leaves on the east side. The leaves were moved on a system of seven trucks at the base of each leaf. Each leaf had thirteen wheels and was driven by five electric motors. A movable seal system between each leaf closed the approximately six-inch space between leaves, keeping rain and snow out and air-conditioning in. The design and manufacture of the drive system was done by a local specialized engineering firm, Heyl and Patterson Inc.

The movable roof system was controlled from a booth located at the top of the seating sections on the east side. The power was supplied to the leaves through wiring in conduits that ran to the top of the building along the cantilever. Each leaf was then fed from the crow's nest that sat at the peak of the roof. Each leaf could be moved individually, which became a problem at one point when one of the operators ran one leaf over the other and damaged the electrical feeds. They could also be moved in unison, which provided the dramatic openings that were done during performances. The roof could be fully opened in about two and a half minutes.

Although intended to accommodate the cultural Civic Light Opera and the Pittsburgh Symphony, the building was truly constructed to handle multipurpose activities. Located under the west-side seating, under three levels of four sections of seating that lifted up, was a full production stage. It was equipped to handle scenery rigging and a full orchestra sound shell. Individual dressing rooms and full cast/team locker rooms were located adjacent to the stage on each side. Rigging the scenery and the shell became expensive, because the system had to be taken down when the seating was retracted back to an arena configuration.

This was one factor that led to the CLO and the symphony moving to other facilities in the 1970s. Another factor was the sound during performances. One of the reasons for the creation of the Civic Arena was to improve the sound, from that played on a temporary outdoor stage at Pitt Stadium to that coming from a facility with better acoustics. Unfortunately, the acoustics of the Arena were still not what the cultural crowd who attended opera, theater and symphonic performances was used to in a closed theater setting. The sound shell and improved sound systems of the day were still not enough to overcome that dilemma.

Another feature that added to the flexibility of the Arena was the retractable seating on the A level. The first thirteen rows of seating from the floor were all either retractable or removable. The seating in front of the stage was removable to accommodate the stage. The balance of seating in that level was retractable to a wall under the B level seats. This allowed for full use of the floor for assorted trade and exhibit shows. It also served the needs of local high schools that held graduations there. It allowed for the graduates to be separated from the audience, which made crowd control easier. The excitement of seeing their child or friend graduate was often overwhelming for some people, and the separation helped keep the peace.

Because of the mammoth size of the roof, a mammoth base was needed to support it. On the west side of the ground floor was a fifty-thousand-square-foot space that came into existence with no dedicated use. A somewhat smaller space existed under the east side seating that accommodated the concession operation, some operating functions and storage for basketball floors, ice floor covers and chairs and tables, as well as vehicle parking. Both ran the entire length of the building from north to south. The west side space became the Exhibit Hall for the city, which at that time had no convention center. That space served multiple uses. In addition to storage and backstage areas for arena shows, it also allowed for home, boat and car shows to have a home. These events took place every year and used the entire Exhibit Hall in addition to the full arena floor area. The hall also served as animal stockyards when circuses came to town; the rodeo used the main floor. It was the dog-grooming area when the Pittsburgh Dog Show was held every spring; it is the biggest dog show in the country outside of Madison Square Garden's Westminster Kennel Club Dog Show. Numerous ski sales, antique shows, coin and stamp shows, gun shows, trade conferences and other events were held in the Exhibit Hall.

One of the advantages of having a retractable roof was that it made additions to the seating capacity fairly simple. The original seating capacity of the arena was approximately 12,000, all in the lower bowl. In the 1970s, many new arenas were adding "super boxes" to their seating configurations. The Penguins decided they needed to add these to increase their revenue sources. Plans were created to add the boxes on the west side of the building over the existing D level seats. The cost and time to do the project was much less with the movable roof, because all the supplies could be lifted by crane into the job rather than bringing the supplies and materials in at ground level then lifting it through existing seating sections. Work was actually completed on the bulk of the facility in about three months over the summer. Shoring had to be added in the Exhibit Hall to accommodate the cranes on the outside terrace of the west side of the building. In the early 1980s, seating was added over two summers to the north and south sides of the building, creating the balconies that took the capacity to 16,500. The same technique was used here, allowing for a time- and cost-effective, economical project. We had to keep an eye on the weather, though, to make sure the interior of the building was not soaked with a sudden summer shower!

This is a shot of the Igloo at night before the final Pitt-Duquesne basketball game at the Civic Arena. The original name of the facility was the Civic Auditorium in 1961, but it was quickly changed to the Civic Arena that year. In 1999, Mellon Financial bought the naming rights, so it became the Mellon Arena. The naming rights expired in its final year. In August 2010, it reverted back to the Civic Arena. *Courtesy of Duquesne Athletics.*

Another unexpected benefit of the movable roof came into play one year when the impeller of the air-conditioning system shattered. On a warm spring day, just prior to the arrival of the annual Shrine Circus, the entire building shook as if an explosion had occurred. The air-conditioning system was unique; only four models like it in the world had ever been built. One of the main pieces was a huge impeller that forced the air out into the system. The impeller, a cast-metal piece about five feet in diameter, was contained in a heavy metal housing. After the impeller shattered, the building engineer, Jack Roberts, started contacting sources to find a replacement. Since only four had ever been made, there were no spares to be found. A replacement was cast. When it was tested, it shattered and blew up the testing building. A second one was cast and passed the test and was installed in early fall, just prior to the commencement of hockey season. All during the preceding summer, we ran events ranging from the circus to World Team Tennis, wrestling matches, concerts and high school graduations. Depending on the event and the weather, we would do openings of the seals only, partial openings of the west side leaves or, occasionally, full openings. We also had to open all the perimeter doors and put fans in each doorway to move air inside the arena seating bowl. It made for a hot summer, but we made it through.

The Civic Arena's roof is its most enduring aspect to the millions of Pittsburghers who entered the facility's gates during the six decades it was open. The roof was a technological masterpiece to not only those patrons but also almost every citizen of western Pennsylvania who had the pleasure to see it during its forty-nine-year run.

WHY THE CIVIC ARENA BECAME THE MELLON ARENA...AND NOT THE MELLON FINANCIAL CENTER

BY TOM ROONEY

Its original name was Civic Auditorium when it opened in 1961. At some early point, for reasons unknown, it began to be referred to as the Civic Arena, a moniker that covered most of its half century of existence. Finally, in 1999 and until it closed in 2010, the facility became known as Mellon Arena. The reason for the last change was simple: money, lots of desperately needed, graciously appreciated money.

I was among the perpetrators of the Mellon Arena name change as president of the Lemieux Group, the operating entity of the Pittsburgh Penguins NHL franchise that called the venue home. I'll share the credit with the following characters.

PNC Bank: "Wha-a-t?" you ask? Well, after PNC announced the naming rights for the new Pirates ballpark, in an exercise of "me too-ism," Mellon Financial was looking for a place to apply its Pittsburgh naming deal.

Marty McGuinn: Chairman and CEO of Mellon Financial, McGuinn already supported the Penguins with a major sponsor that bordered on sheer benevolence given the sad state of the team, which was skating on the thinnest of financial ice. He wanted to respond to PNC's Pirates claim. Additionally, the Mellon Financial brand had interests in many of the markets where the Penguins played on the road. And games broadcast back to those markets from Pittsburgh would reinforce that recognition.

During the Penguins' Stanley Cup run in 2009, the team set up a large screen outside the Civic Arena for fans who were unable to buy tickets, allowing them to be able to be part of the atmosphere and watch the games. Since then, it has become a playoff tradition for the team. *Courtesy of Rich Boyer.*

Mario Lemieux: He stepped up to buy the team, which could have been headed out of town. And it was Mario's appeal to Mellon Financial that resonated with McGuinn.

Jim Lauteri: Mellon Financial's brand manager was tasked by McGuinn to justify the deal.

Tom Rooney/Dave Soltesz: Dave, our vice-president of sales, ably worked up the justification for the big ask we had in mind.

So, Mario, Marty, Jim and I were in the Mellon Financial office tower, and we went through the presentation. Marty says to Mario, "Let's go for lunch, Mario, we'll let Jim and Tom here work out the details."

Sweet. Jim and I worked out the details with our staffs, and we got a huge financial lift.

It wasn't an easy transition. To get around using the Mellon name, the *New York Times* hockey beat writer referred to games in Pittsburgh as occurring at the "Igloo," a commonly used nickname for the building given its appearance from the outside, especially on snowy nights when the Pens were playing. Appeals to the writer that the money for the naming rights was vital to the team seemed to hit home. And it got McGuinn off my

27

back. A common McGuinn phone call to me went like this: "Tom, they're [insert media entity] calling it Civic Arena (or the Igloo) again. Paying a lot of money for this."

Oh, and there's one more person to thank.

Steve Reich: Steve was Mario's agent. Marty McGuinn initially directed that the arena be called Mellon Financial Arena instead of Mellon Arena. "Marty," Steve said in a followup meeting, "the First Union Center in Philadelphia is sarcastically referred to as the F.U. Center. If you name it Mellon Financial Arena, inevitably some people will call it the M.F. Arena." McGuinn thought for a second and said, "Come to think of it, I do like the name Mellon Arena."

TEAR THE ROOF OFF THE SUCKER

CREATING A COLLECTIBLE ORNAMENT
FORGED FROM THE CIVIC ARENA ROOF

BY CHRIS FLETCHER

When the announcement came that the Mellon (née Civic) Arena was to be torn down, a serious question was on the minds of all fans of hockey, basketball, truck pulls, circuses, ice-skating events and concerts: With the loss of the Igloo, would Pittsburgh be giving up the funk? Memorable buildings are more than concrete and steel. They have soul. Or, as that great philosopher George Clinton said, they have funk. They help create one Penguins nation under a groove.

After all, the building had a real type of thing going down, getting down, a whole lot of rhythm going 'round. And that was true whether it was sports, music or other live entertainment. As any Pittsburgher embedded on the Mothership would tell you, we gotta have that funk. Only the evil Sir Nose D'Voidoffunk would argue that point.

The Mellon/Civic Arena evolved into an awkward building with seats and suites crammed in every conceivable nook and cranny. There were seats for hockey where fans couldn't see the ice if they stood up. (I watched Mario's first game returning from retirement in one of them.) Its tight concourses restricted revenue generation, and in the money-first era of sports entertainment, that meant the place was obsolete.

That doesn't mean the decision was greeted warmly in all circles, nor was there agreement on what to do with the body, especially since it had historical value. The demise of the Arena brought great tension between preservationists and developers. Preservationists wanted to incorporate

Cory Bonnet is an artist from Pittsburgh who creates spectacular pieces from salvaging parts of buildings that have been torn down. He used panels from the Civic Arena roof to paint these masterpieces. This picture of the Arena shows just how magnificent the facility was. *Courtesy of Cory Bonnet.*

parts of the existing building into any new development plans. Renowned Pittsburgh architect Rob Pfaffman was a vocal critic of just demolishing the facility. He, along with Preservation Pittsburgh president Scott Lieb, advocated a creative reuse solution. Among the ideas was using the supports on which the roof was placed as the framing for a park that looked into the city's downtown. But the Penguins, who held development rights, quickly nixed that idea. What both camps wanted was a new multiuse facility that allowed for adjacent development and that would have a sense of excitement—or funk.

Entering into this fray came a partial solution that checked off a lot of boxes. It would salvage one of the more notable elements of the building—its silver roof, which was made more spectacular by a deep cleaning in the early 1980s. It would honor the history of the building by letting fans have a keepsake piece of the arena. It would allow a local business to create a signature piece. And perhaps most important, it would have a charitable aspect.

Wendell August Forge in Grove City had been making hand-crafted metal gifts for nearly a century. The company had built its business on creating iconic Pittsburgh scenes—the skyline, the Incline, the Golden Triangle and more—on coasters and serving trays. Chances are you or someone you know has one of its pieces. But if it wasn't for the Penguins, the company would not have survived. Its die would have been cast.

In 2010, Wendell August won a bid to produce a fundraising commemorative piece for the team that would benefit the Pittsburgh Penguins Foundation. The item was a replica ticket stamped in aluminum. The company had never made the item before, but as it had through so much of its history, it turned to its skilled metal artisans to create a design. The deal with the Penguins represented the largest order in the forge's history. They were going to cap it full.

But as the company was on the verge of success, three days after signing the deal, disaster struck. The Wendell August Forge building, constructed in the 1930s mostly out of wood, burned to the ground. Firefighters were unable to stop the blaze, but they were able to save some of the company's dies that had been used to forge its products. Penguins Foundation president Dave Soltez heard about the fire on the news and immediately reached out to Wendell August's management team. When he found out that the die for the ticket survived, he assured the forge company that the team planned on honoring the order. After all, the Penguins knew something about rising from the ashes—being padlocked by the IRS and nearly losing the franchise more than once. Not only would the foundation keep the project, but it would also pay the contract in full, upfront, allowing Wendell August the ability to buy supplies and keep production going in a makeshift operation within a week. The Pens, in essence, said, "Let's take it to the stage."

Given that history, when it came time to find a good reuse solution for the roof, there was no debate as to who the vendor would be. The materials presented a bit of a challenge. There were three different gauges of steel, each of which had weathered a bit differently and had various patinas.

The foundation and forge exchanged ideas before settling on a keepsake ornament that would feature the Arena and the Penguins logo. From there, the artisans went to work. They created a die—drawn backward so that the image would show the right way when finished. Each ornament was hand cut and handmade. But first, ya gotta shake the gate. A piece of the arena roof was clamped to a table, where a PSI hydraulic hammer carefully followed the die, tracing the intricate design. Those patinas on the roof turned out to be a good thing, as each piece became a one-of-a-kind collector's item.

In 1964, Duquesne University moved its men's basketball program to the Civic Arena. That season, one of the greatest players in the program's history, Willie Somerset (*left*), was entering his senior year. He went on to a fabulous professional career in both the ABA and NBA, where he averaged 21.9 points per game. The school eventually retired his number. *Courtesy of Duquesne Athletics.*

Demand for the ornaments was so heavy that eleven thousand were sold in the first twenty-four hours. The foundation could only guarantee that fifteen thousand would be delivered by Christmas. Like elves, the artisans worked. But the roof would continue to supply both inspiration and products for the partnership. Coasters, awards, trays and more came from the roof before the supply of metal eventually ran out.

But Wendall August Forge blew the roof off the sucker. In all, the company produced products that netted more than $1 million for the Penguins Foundation. That money funded youth hockey in western Pennsylvania. It connected fans to the Arena, where so many hockey memories were made. And it preserved the funk.

5

THE CIVIC ARENA DOME STILL SHINES IN CORY BONNET'S ART

BY TOM ROONEY

Hardly out of Gateway High School, George Boehm had just started at Noralco Corporation in Pittsburgh when he was sent out to a job to help with the demolition of Forbes Field. Someone handed him a crescent wrench. "Unbolt the seats," the foreman said. "Which ones?" George asked. "All of them," said the boss. Well, George did have some help, and that job would start a one-stop career of forty-eight years that included site work to prepare for the construction of both PNC Park and Heinz Field, as well as the teardown of the Civic Arena, where an artist named Cory Bonnet relentlessly hounded him about sharing some of the iconic stainless-steel panels that made up the famous dome of the place known affectionately by locals as the "Igloo."

"At every demo site people show up with ideas or to beg for stuff," Boehm recalled. "They can be a nuisance, really. We had a lot invested there and we loved our employees. I'd tell everyone if 30 guys start a job each morning I wanted 30 to go home safe that night. It can be dangerous. We didn't need scavenger hunters."

But George took a liking to Cory, and the rest is history—preserving history. "You know, other than that dome, the Arena was a pretty ordinary building," George recalled. "Cory wouldn't stop calling. The only way I could get rid of him was to give him what he wanted! But with every demolition you know you're tearing down someone's living memory. I wanted people to come away with something anyway."

In Game 2 of the 1991 Stanley Cup Finals, Mario Lemieux had perhaps the signature goal of his Hall of Fame career. He called for a pass from teammate Phil Bourque, slid the puck past two defensemen, then made an incredible move on Star goaltender Jon Casey, depositing the puck in the net. Artist Cory Bonnet does a spectacular job of capturing that moment in this piece. *Courtesy of Cory Bonnet.*

Cory Bonnet had a passion for history and for using his considerable talent and skill to preserve it for posterity—for the public and for private enjoyment. Whether it's the Arena pieces, some doors from the Produce Terminal in Pittsburgh's Strip District, wood used as steel ingot molds from a Homestead steel mill, pews from closed holy spaces like Saints Peter and Paul Church in the city's East Liberty neighborhood, Bonnet steps through the clutter and steps into preserving some of the elements that gave his beloved Pittsburgh region its character. "I'm fascinated with Pittsburgh's gritty and maybe even grimy past," Bonnet said. "We're a very different city, literally and figuratively, than where our grandparents lived and we should never forget where we came from."

Clients even bring their own recycled materials. One family wanted a painting on an outhouse door from their original homestead. "These are very successful people who are grounded enough to remember their humble roots," he said. A similar project involved using the top of a card table that had been at a summer cottage for decades. "They wanted something to remember those gin rummy games played by generations of the same family at that tabletop."

For the Arena project, Bonnet secured three four-by-seven-foot steel panels, the largest he could secure in his SUV. He sawed them into workable shapes and sizes, laid them out in his driveway like a giant tanning bed, washed them with everyday soap and let them dry in the sun. They were accustomed to having the sun reflected off them for fifty years at the Civic Arena. "I wanted some of the original patina and scratches to survive to really represent their original life," he said.

When Bonnet peered into the panels, it was a mystical experience. "I could see myself reflected going to the Arena as a boy the first time," he said. "Walking down those steel steps from the upper parking lot on a bitter cold night, the dome-lit glowing, it looked like a spaceship against the skyline. The massive steel arm reminded me of a mooring mast. It looked unreal. I saw it again in my driveway."

Inspiration also came from some great photos the late Bob Dorsett provided Cory. Dorsett was eyewitness to many of the magic moments as a forty-year member of the Stagehands Union in Pittsburgh.

Bonnet's process involves some meditation. "I stare a lot. Eventually the material presents a vision, although sometimes it can be instantaneous," he said. He continues to collect materials and a network has developed of people wanting to save things precious in their memories. "I have stuff everywhere…all waiting their turn," he said.

Waiting their turn. Like George Boehm's turn of the crescent wrench on his first job in the demolition of Forbes Field. "Thank goodness for people like George that have a heart," Bonnet said. "The Civic Arena produced a half century of memories…Mario Lemieux, Muhammad Ali, music from Michael Jackson to Metallica, ice shows, circuses and every form of sports and entertainment. It made memories and I'm glad to help preserve them."

Cory's art lives on the internet, too, at www.corybonnet.com.

PART II

HOCKEY

6

1967 PENGUINS (TRY TO) TAKE FLIGHT IN PITTSBURGH

BY TOM ROONEY

Contrary to the chapter title, penguins don't fly. They are in fact by definition a flightless bird.

And they didn't actually take Pittsburgh by storm that first season, 1967–68. Some cynical hardcore hockey fans were known to bellow "bring back the Hornets" after another of the many Penguin losses, especially by midseason. The Hornets were in reference to the minor-league team that had vacated the Civic Arena the year before to make way for the big-time National Hockey League Penguins. Those Hornets went out in style with the American Hockey League's Calder Cup championship, the poor man's Stanley Cup.

I didn't follow the Hornets. My neighbors on the North Side tried to get me to go to a game. But I was a certifiable sports snob. We had major-league teams to watch in the Pirates and Steelers, although the latter were almost laughable losers. And because my dad was a ticket-sales guy for the Rooney family business, I'd often have a wad of free tickets to pass out on my paper route. A couple of times I even got beat up trying to give them away.

But I went from ice cold to red hot for hockey following those first-year Penguins. When I couldn't get to a game or it was on the road, I'd have it playing on the store radio at a Bard's Dairyland location near my North Side home, trying to catch Ed Conway's play-by-play between slicing baked ham or measuring "walkaway sundaes," miniature versions of the regular thing, doled out in a cone-shaped cup.

I really got lucky in 1968 when I started college. I became an usher at the Arena. Imagine, for the next four years I would be paid to watch the games. Then I spent ten years with the DeBartolo Corporation, running the Arena and promoting the team in the 1980s. My "hat trick" with the franchise was achieved when I came back from Texas in 1999 to be president of Lemieux Group, Mario's consortium that rescued the franchise from flying (waddling?) the coop.

Years after my ushering career, I became friends with some of the cast of characters involved with the embryonic Pens. Jack Riley was their first general manager, and we became particularly close in my last involvement. General Manager Craig Patrick, at my gentle nudge, made Jack his GM emeritus. Joe Gordon, who would be recognized as the premier NFL PR man with the "Super '70s Steelers," became my frequent lunch partner at Atria's in Mount Lebanon with Riley. Another at the big corner table was

Shown here is the statue of the Pittsburgh Steelers' legendary owner, Art Rooney, "the Chief," that stands outside of Heinz Field. In 1967, the NHL was looking to add six more teams, and the final slot looked like it was between Pittsburgh and Buffalo. With Buffalo looking like it had the advantage, one of the potential Pittsburgh owners, Jack McGregor, asked Rooney to see if he could change the mind of Chicago's James Norris, who was in favor of Buffalo. Rooney used his influence to do just that, and the Penguins soon were born. *Courtesy of David Finoli.*

Bill Heufelder, the first beat writer covering the team for the *Pittsburgh Press*. We often talked early Pens.

"I wasn't too crazy about the name 'Penguins' when that won the name-the-team contest," Riley once told me. "But I had a lot more to worry about than that. The Hornets had left as very popular champs to the core nucleus of fans we had for hockey in Pittsburgh. Our owners felt we had to win early, and it really influenced that first roster, which was mostly veteran players I hoped would still have something in the tank."

The NHL had doubled its league in 1966 by adding six teams; Pittsburgh, Philadelphia Flyers, Minnesota North Stars, St. Louis Blues, Oakland Seals and Los Angeles Kings. They joined defending Stanley Cup champs Toronto Maple Leafs, Montreal Canadiens, Boston Bruins, New York Rangers, Detroit Red Wings and Chicago Blackhawks. The newcomers began play in the fall of '67.

Pittsburgh very nearly didn't make the cut for the first expansion, but Steelers owner Art Rooney, a hockey fan himself, lobbied NHL owners he knew. Pittsburgh got the last of the six spots over Buffalo.

"I was standing at the old teletype machine at the *Press*, waiting for the announcement," said Heufelder, who grew up watching Gordie Howe in Detroit. Heufelder came to Pittsburgh a few years earlier from a small daily near Milwaukee. "Nobody wanted the minor league hockey beat, so I covered the Hornets for two years....And then came the news on the wire. I felt like I hit the lottery."

Riley decided the Pens had to jump-start into the NHL, so he asked the league to have the vaunted Canadiens play the Penguins in their first game. Montreal was in a stretch of winning ten Stanley Cups in twenty years in the 1950s and '60s. Riley remembered: "The league asked, 'Are you sure, what if you get slaughtered?' I thought it was worth it, maybe catch Montreal in a little still-training-camp mode."

The Pens nearly pulled off a sensational upset, losing 2–1 to the "Habs" before 9,307 fans on October 11. Andy Bathgate was thirty-four, long in the tooth for a hockey player and a poster child reclamation project for Riley's largely over-the-hill hockey squad. Bathgate, a Hall of Famer for his earlier exploits, scored the Pens' first goal that night. He was a handsome guy in the days when hardly any player wore helmets, and his perfectly coiffed black hair was peppered with gray. He always wore a trendy black turtleneck under his blue-and-white uniform. After a pretty good autumn, age, injuries and a lack of depth kicked in, and the Penguins missed the playoffs despite winning their last four games at season's end.

"They had very little depth, and when their number one pick in the expansion draft, Earl Ingarfield, went down with a serious knee injury, they started to stumble," Heufelder remembered. "Teams like Philadelphia and Los Angeles had bought their own farm clubs (Quebec City and Springfield, Massachusetts, respectively), and they could restock. I think the Pens had like two minor leaguers. A guy who made the team in training camp, Jeannot Gilbert, actually walked into Jack's office the day before the season and asked to be sent back to the minor-league Hershey team. That tells you about their prospects."

Heufelder recalled that first training camp in Ontario and how the team of recycled veterans had to mold into a squad. Bathgate, whom he described as "the nicest pro athlete he ever covered," tried to keep it loose. "Pittsburgh had this really short winger, Billy Dea, and after an exhibition game in a dungy old arena somewhere, the players were in this common shower with a board around the edges. Water was starting to rise because of all the guys, and Bathgate said to Dea, 'Hey, Billy, watch you don't drown in here.'"

The reliance on older players made a rebound season impossible the next year. "They were never a serious playoff contender those first two years," Heufelder remembered. "The worst thing that could happen happened… they had to follow a Hornets team people still loved. Poor Jack Riley, the old guys had run out of gas."

7

THE DEFINITION OF BALANCED SCORING

THE 1974-75 PENGUINS

BY PAUL ALEXANDER

For those of you scoring at home, the Pittsburgh Penguins did indeed exist prior to the arrival of Mario Lemieux. It was in their eighth season of existence that the Pens actually made a little noise in their home building. The Civic Arena, fondly referred to as the Igloo, played host to a pretty good hockey club. There was no threat of sellout records or even any social distancing issues, but the Penguins were fun to watch.

The 1974–75 season marked the Penguins' first in the Norris Division of the Prince of Wales Conference. They had tremendous talent in first-round draft pick Pierre Larouche and a skilled and talented top six that scored an impressive 326 goals in the regular season.

Those old enough will remember the incredible Jean Pronovost and the somewhat iconic chant, "Let's Go Pronovost." He led the team in goals with 43 that season and became the first Penguin to 300 career points. Pronie also became the first to wear the blue Penguin sweater in five hundred games.

The lightly regarded Penguins had nine players who scored 20 or more goals that season and nine who registered 50 or more points for the year. That offensive production propelled the Pens to a third appearance in the postseason and put them in a position to make a deep run toward the Stanley Cup. Until the Pens' lofty accomplishment, only two other teams in NHL history had more than nine players topping the 20-goal plateau in a single season; the 1970–71 Boston Bruins and the Montreal

While the Penguins came very close to turning the corner in 1975, their dreams of a Stanley Cup were trashed after the New York Islanders came back from a three-games-to-none deficit to stun the Pens in the second round. Eventually, they would get that title and then some. Shown here is Sidney Crosby hoisting the Cup during a Stanley Cup championship parade down Grant Street in Pittsburgh after the team won its fifth title in 2017. *Courtesy of David Finoli.*

Canadiens in this season, both with ten players. It was the true definition of balanced scoring.

For the team, it was their first campaign finishing over .500 for a season. Their 89-point total remained the high-water mark until 1992–93, when they accumulated a franchise record 119 points to capture their one and only Presidents' Trophy, emblematic of the highest regular-season point total in the league. Remarkably, in their first two Stanley Cup championship years, they failed to top the 89-point plateau.

The electric Ron Schock led the way with a team-high 86 points that included a team record for assists in a season with 63. The silky smooth Syl Apps Jr. put up 79 points as he became the first Penguin to 200 career assists. Ron Stackhouse set a new standard among Pittsburgh defensemen with 45 assists and 60 points. Paul Coffey and Kris LeTang had to break someone's records.

Lucky Pierre made the scouts look great by establishing Penguin rookie records of 31 goals and 68 points. Larouche also represented the Prince of Wales Conference in Montreal at the NHL All-Star Game. Pittsburgh was well represented. Pronovost and Apps were also selected, and Apps was named the game's Most Valuable Player. Keep in mind, Pittsburgh was far from a hockey town at this point. In fact, that memorable season was almost one of the Penguins' last in Pittsburgh.

It's hard to say how many people would've noticed or even objected if the NHL's plans to relocate two of the league's underachievers had come to fruition. The Penguins and the California Golden Seals were scheduled to be moved. The Penguins were to become the Seattle Totems but were bought out from under the would-be Seattle owner for $4.4 million in bankruptcy court.

The Penguins were opening some eyes and actually getting noticed throughout the NHL and, more important, in their hometown. Averaging a somewhat modest (by league standards) 11,222 fans per game, the cultlike fan base still had a team to cheer for. This was a pretty talented group that had a penchant for lighting the lamp.

Pittsburgh was enjoying its best season since the Penguins' inception in 1967 and was becoming a legitimate franchise. Their third trip to the playoffs was one that many will never forget, but not for the right reasons. After dispatching the St. Louis Blues with two straight wins in the opening-round best-of-three series, the Penguins made a little history.

In the quarterfinals, the Penguins jumped out to a three-games-to-none lead on the New York Islanders. Only one other team in NHL history had managed to come back from a three-to-nothing deficit: the 1942 Toronto Maple Leafs. Islander head coach Al Arbor challenged his team and told them that if they didn't think they could win four straight, they should get off the ice. New York stormed back with three straight wins. All that was left was Game 7 in Pittsburgh.

Ed Westfall broke a scoreless tie with just five minutes left in the third period. Chico Resch sealed the deal with the shutout, and the seeds of that Islander dynasty were firmly planted. New York Islander historians say that it was that playoff run that fell short that was the impetus for four straight Stanley Cups beginning in 1979.

For the Penguins, it was certainly a season from which to build, and while they enjoyed a modicum of success to close out the decade, it wasn't until a last-place finish in 1983–84 that they were in position to draft an all-time great in Mario Lemieux.

That 1974–75 season appeared to have all of the stars aligned. The stat sheet was filled with big numbers. Franchise records were established for wins and points in a season. There was an amazing rookie talent in Pierre Larouche. These Penguins were playing a very entertaining style of hockey with 20-plus goal scorers sprinkled throughout the roster. Hockey had finally been noticed in Pittsburgh, and history had been made.

8

LUCKY PIERRE

THE PENGUINS' FIRST GATE ATTRACTION

BY JOHN WDOWIAK

On February 2, 1974, the Pittsburgh Penguins lost, 3–1, to the Chicago Blackhawks at the Civic Arena. Ron Lalonde scored the Pens' only goal. The famed "Century Line" of Lowell MacDonald, Syl Apps and Jean Pronovost finished a minus 3. Only four penalty minutes were charged to each team, which meant that everyone was downright civil to one another, at least according to 1970s hockey.

Seems like an otherwise meaningless loss in a season that saw forty-one of them, but it wasn't really. For me, it was everything, because it was my first NHL game in person. I was three days away from my eleventh birthday and already obsessed with a sport that I had never even played. Although too young to realize it at the time, while I was watching the Pens lose that night, I was already a suffering fan. I saw players like Stan Mikita, Tony Esposito and Dale Tallon skate around my heroes, and I couldn't help but wish the Penguins had stars like them. For my birthday, I wanted just one thing: I wanted the Penguins to be winners.

The Penguins finished the 1973–74 season with a record of 28-41-9, good for 65 points and the eighth overall pick in the NHL entry draft. They were eyeing an eighteen-year-old French Canadian star who had shattered scoring records in the Quebec Major Junior League (QMJHL). Sound familiar? So, on June 12, 1974, the Penguins selected Pierre Larouche, an offensive juggernaut known for his flair as much as for his scoring touch. In his last

As the Penguins returned to the Stanley Cup Finals in 2008, Ryan Malone (12), shown tipping in a shot against the Philadelphia Flyers, was a pivotal part of the team, scoring a career-high 27 goals that season. *Courtesy of David Finoli.*

season playing in the QMJHL, Larouche had 94 goals and 157 assists for a total 251 points—in one season. Now he was a Pittsburgh Penguin. Maybe my birthday wish had come true.

In 1974, the Pittsburgh Pirates were just three years removed from winning a World Series with Willie Stargell and the Lumber Company. The Steelers finished 10-3-1 on their way to winning their first Super Bowl in January 1975. The Pitt football team finished 7-4 and ranked twentieth in the country. The Penguins? Nobody was really talking about them. They were fighting for the Pittsburgh consumer sports dollar; they needed to win, and they needed to do it with style. Enter Lucky Pierre.

When Larouche landed at Greater Pittsburgh International Airport, it was the first time he had been on an airplane. Pittsburghese? Larouche didn't even speak English. But he was a young, flashy player with good looks and charm who scored goals in bunches. That was enough for the Penguins to make him the centerpiece of their team both on and off the ice.

In a *New York Times* article of November 7, 1983, the Penguins' director of news media relations, Terry Schiffhauer, said: "It was incredible, the way he had this town in the palm of his hand. I really think that before long he would have been the biggest thing this town ever had. Bigger than Bradshaw. Bigger than Clemente.'"

There was even a "Win-a-Date-with-Pierre Contest." More than fifteen thousand women entered. To hear Larouche tell it, though, he didn't really understand or realize what was happening on the business side of a fledgling NHL team.

"I really wasn't aware that I was being drafted as a 'marquee' player. It didn't enter my mind," he said. "When you're on the ice…when you're playing, you just play. Honestly, I was just hoping to get drafted. They would book me for appearances and promotions. We were trying to promote hockey and the team. It was fun."

If he was having fun off the ice, then what Larouche did on the ice qualified as an outright celebration. As a rookie, he had 31 goals and 37 assists in 79 games. The Penguins finished that 1974–75 season with a record of 37-28-15 for 89 points. That was nine more wins than the previous year without Larouche and 24 more points. The next year, he had 111 points, including 53 goals, making him the first Penguin to record 100 points in a season and the youngest NHL player to score 50 goals in a season. In fact, Larouche notched his 100th point at the Civic Arena on March 24, 1976, in a 5–5 tie against the Boston Bruins. In that same game, Pronovost became the first Penguin to score 50 goals in a season. Less than two weeks later, on April 3, 1976, also at the Civic Arena, Lucky Pierre joined the 50-goal club when he scored twice in a 5–4 loss to the Washington Capitals.

While those early years were filled with promise, it wasn't just the on-ice accomplishments that Larouche remembers. "One of the things that sticks out was the language barrier," Larouche explained. "It took me 4–5 months just to understand a sentence. I remember there was a restaurant I used to go to and their menu had pictures of the food. That was perfect for me. I could just point to the thing I wanted. Years later, after I was more comfortable with the language, I went back to that restaurant and was able to order by just saying what I wanted."

Today, Larouche's LinkedIn page says he's been a "Corporate Sales Liaison" with the Penguins since 1999. When you ask him what the job entails, he replies: "I've known Mario [Lemieux] a long time. We're friends. It's that simple. When he needs something, when he needs help, I'm there for him. He asks me questions and I give him answers. I tell him what I think. He knows I won't hold back. We talk and it seems we're able to figure things out. I just love being part of it."

Giving advice to the Penguin owner and player who broke nearly all of his QMJHL records—Larouche's single-season total of 157 assists still stands as the benchmark—isn't the only counseling that Larouche does. After all, he knows a little something about being a rookie with high expectations.

"I don't necessarily share my specific experiences with young players today because it was a different time when I came into the league, but there's still things that I can do to help," Larouche says. "I'm trying to encourage them, to keep them in the right mindset and tell them to keep plugging. I'll do or say whatever they need to help them keep working toward being successful."

He does it because, although that first season as a tantalizing rookie with star power is a distant memory, it's not completely forgotten. "There's always a moment that still happens and then I remember dreaming as a kid. There are still moments that make me think about how my hands and feet were freezing when I was on a rink as a kid in Quebec," he said. "Or maybe there's something that makes me think about my first NHL game versus the Minnesota North Stars. I've been fortunate. I'll never forget that."

9

TANKS FOR THE MEMORIES

THE 1983-84 PENGUINS' QUEST
TO FINISH LAST

BY CHRIS FLETCHER

It wasn't easy being a Pittsburgh Penguin fan in 1983–84. They were god-awful, more AHL than NHL. They drew about 6,000 fans—on a good night. About the only positive thing I could say living in an apartment with a view of the Civic Arena was that I knew I could buy a cheap ticket, slip the usher a tenner and find myself in a seat behind the glass. That is, if I could stomach watching the shit show starring such players as Pat Boutette, Gary Rissling, Rod Buskas and Greg Fox. They were to professional hockey what velvet Elvis paintings were to art.

By Christmas, it was apparent that the playoffs were out of the question and the Pens should do what all terrible teams do—focus on next year. Usually, that means a roster shakeup that gives management an opportunity to see what they have in terms of talent in the minors, scouring other teams for possible trades at the deadline, ranking upcoming free agents and preparing for the draft.

But the Penguins took that last one to the extreme. They knew that the team that finished dead last would get the opportunity of a generation—no, make that of a lifetime. They would get to select Mario Lemieux as the first pick. Lemieux was already a legend. In the juniors in Laval, Quebec, he was giving notice that he was the top amateur player in the world, notching a mind-blowing 282 points in 70 games. The Penguins decided the best course of action was to lose as many games as possible to ensure that Lemieux would be wearing their sweater.

And so, they tanked, although not officially. Yet, if Webster's had a picture for the entry for *tank* (a verb meaning to make no effort to win; to lose intentionally), you'd see a Pens logo along with photos of Eddie "E.J." Johnston and Lou Angotti. The Pens were led by these two longtime hockey guys. General Manager E.J. had played goalie for some successful Boston Bruin teams. Head coach Angotti was the original captain of the Philadelphia Flyers. E.J., to this day, vehemently denies tanking. Angotti contradicts him and admits he did everything he could to ensure a last-place finish.

It's hard to doubt Angotti. The team shuffled its roster, with forty-eight players lacing up skates for the Pens during the campaign. That's almost enough to field three merely shitty teams instead of one historically bad one. Johnston traded away defenseman and captain Randy Carlyle, two years removed from a Norris Trophy season, receiving a future first-round draft pick and a player to be named later. His name was Moe Mantha.

Pittsburgh Penguin owners Mario Lemieux (*left*) and Ron Burkle (*right*) wave to the fans during the parade to celebrate the Stanley Cup championship that the team won in 2009. Since buying the team, the two owners have led the team to three Stanley Cup championships and helped bring a new arena to the city. *Courtesy of David Finoli.*

Then there was the coaching. Angotti would often send out his fourth line against opponents' top lines. He filled his penalty-killing lines with defensive liabilities. When rookie goalie Roberto Romano started to find his groove and put together a winning streak, he was promptly shipped to the minors in Baltimore. He was replaced by Vincent Trembley, rumored to be working as a milk deliveryman at the time of his call-up. Trembley started four games, posting an "impressive" goals against average of 6.0.

Angotti tells the story of being berated by Johnston when the team jumped out to a 3–0 lead against the Rangers. "What the hell are you trying to do?" he steamed. "You're going to blow this!"

And they almost did, thanks to the New Jersey Devils, who were nearly as inept. The Devils were in their second year of existence in New Jersey after moving from Colorado and had the talent level of an expansion team, so they at least had an excuse for being so bad. The two bottom feeders met the final time on March 6, 1984, in New Jersey. Never had so much ridden on the results of a game between such awful hockey teams. The Devils' Bob Hoffmeyer broke a 3–3 tie early in the third on the way to an eventual 6–5 Devil win in regulation.

E.J. sighed in relief. Can you imagine losing on purpose all season long and not getting the prize? Had the Penguins won this game, they would have ended the season with 40 points, the Devils with 39, instead of the Devils' 41 and the Penguins' 38. The Penguins ended up winning by losing.

They built around Lemieux, adding Hall of Famers Ron Francis, Joe Mullen, Paul Coffey and Larry Murphy as well as stars like Jaromir Jagr, Tom Barrasso, Kevin Stevens and Ulf Sammuelson. They ushered in the first golden era of Penguin hockey, along with two Stanley Cup championships. Unfortunately for the architects of the tanking, neither would be there for the ultimate glory. Angotti was fired the next season and, because of his complicity, would never be an NHL head coach again. E.J. was gone three years before the first cup, but his fingerprints were all over it.

But none of that could have happened without the great tanking. When the Ottawa Senators tried a similar approach to land Alexander Daigle a decade later, the NHL stepped in and instituted a draft lottery.

But back to 1983–84 and the Penguins cheating to lose. I don't know that I could argue with the strategy. Would you rather sacrifice one season for the future (more on that in a second)? Was E.J. doing right by being morally wrong?

I say yes, particularly if we peer into an alternate universe where it's the Devils that finish with the worst record. In this world, the Penguins have to settle for a good but not great player with the second pick of the draft. They choose Kirk Muller, who would play more than 1,300 games and score 357 goals and 602 assists—about half of Lemieux's output.

The Penguins without a true star wither and die and are then sold off to a group in Kansas City. The fall is so ugly that even when the NHL is looking for expansion opportunities, the league passes on Pittsburgh. Its fan base is not strong enough to warrant a second chance.

Meanwhile, in New Jersey, they are raising their first Stanley Cup in 1989–90. Lemieux is a perennial all-star, and the team becomes a dynasty with the addition of goaltender Martin Brodeur and defenseman Scott Niedermayer (dead).

Then there is the effect on the NHL. With their balance of offense and defense, there's no need for the Devils to resort to neutral zone trapping. As a result, the clutch-and-grab era of the NHL never happens. Scoring remains high, and fan interest in the game explodes with the advent of high-definition television.

The NHL once again looks to expand, but Pittsburgh is again passed over because of the aging Civic Arena. Without a new facility, the league instead awards a franchise to tech-hub Seattle, and hockey becomes the sport of choice in the Pacific Northwest.

Sidney Crosby? Never a Penguin. No Evgeni Malkin or Marc Andre Fleury, either. Pittsburgh is not recognized as the best hockey city in America. High school hockey exists at only a few schools. The Stanley Cup never rests at the bottom of Mario's Sewickley pool during a celebration. The Cup never travels to Pittsburgh. PPG Paints Arena never happens.

So, was it worth it to tank? You're goddamn right it was.

10

LORD STANLEY, LORD STANLEY, GIVE ME THE BRANDY

THE CHAMPIONSHIP ERA BEGINS

BY JOHN WDOWIAK

On October 4, 1990, the Pittsburgh Pirates beat the Cincinnati Reds, 4–3, to take a 1–0 lead in the National League Championship Series. It was the first time the Pirates had been in the playoffs since 1979, and just like that, there was hope again for Steel City sports fans.

The next night, the Penguins were beginning their 1990–91 season with a 7–4 win at the Washington Capitals. Two days later, the home campaign opened with a repeat score—again, a 7–4 victory—this time over the New Jersey Devils at the Civic Arena. Among the goal scorers was Jaromir Jagr, an eighteen-year-old rookie who scored his first NHL goal—the game-winner no less.

Unfortunately, a short week later, the Pirates were out of the playoffs, having lost the series, 4–2, to the Reds. A streak of twenty years with a losing record was just around the corner. For the Penguins, 1990–91 was the beginning of a different streak. It was the beginning of a run in which they missed the playoffs only four times in the next twenty-eight seasons and produced five Stanley Cup championships.

Although that first Stanley Cup season wasn't exactly the start of the Penguins' style of high-scoring hockey, they certainly used their potent offense that year to cement their place as a team whose defensive philosophy could be described as, "If you score 6 goals, we'll score 7." If you were keeping a scorebook during games at the Civic Arena that year, you should

After missing most of the regular season in 1990–91 for the Penguins, Joe Mullen returned
to the team in the playoffs and helped the franchise win its first Stanley Cup title. Mullen
became the first American-born player to score 500 goals in a career, as well as 1,000 points.
Mullen was a favorite to be part of the famed 1980 USA gold-medal team but decided to
turn pro instead. *Courtesy of Boston College Athletics.*

Born in the same hometown as boxing legend Rocky Marciano—Brockton, Massachusetts—Kevin Stevens became one of the greatest players in Pittsburgh Penguin history after his rights were traded from the Los Angeles Kings following the 1983 NHL Draft. A product of Boston College, Stevens went on to score 54 and 55 goals in back-to-back seasons for Pittsburgh between 1991 and 1993. *Courtesy of Boston College Athletics.*

have brought some extra pages. Here's just a few of the memorable games from the regular season:

10/25/90   *A 6–3 win over Quebec in which Kevin Stevens had a hat trick, the first of five on the season for the team scored by five different players.*

12/13/90   *Nine different players scored as the Pens beat the New Jersey Devils, 9–5, on only 32 shots.*

12/18/90   *They must have liked the number 9, because they scored 9 again just five days later against Winnipeg, this time with eight different scorers.*

12/28/90   *Their lone shutout of the year, a 5–0 victory over the Detroit Red Wings, in which Tom Barrasso stopped 27 shots.*

No doubt the talent was there. A prized rookie in Jagr; elite veterans such as Ron Francis, Joey Mullen, Larry Murphy and Ulf Samuelsson; experienced Stanley Cup winners such as Bryan Trottier and Paul Coffey; and a core led by Mario Lemieux, Stevens and Mark Recchi, all of whom desperately wanted to win a Cup. But all that talent had to be brought together for eighty regular-season games just to get to the playoffs. Enter Bob Johnson.

Before he came to Pittsburgh, Johnson's professional résumé was five seasons as head coach of the Calgary Flames, where they made just one playoff appearance. From 1987 to 1990, he served as president of USA Hockey, which meant that, when he got to Pittsburgh, Johnson had been away from the professional game for three years.

It didn't matter. In an interview for the Penguins' fiftieth-anniversary documentary, longtime team announcer and marketing executive Paul Steigerwald said of "Badger" Bob: "His power as a human being is what made him a great coach. It was his ability to exude that passion that he had for the game and transfer it to you." In the same interview, Recchi put it a little more simply: "He was the best coach I ever had."

So Johnson took his stars, grinders, fourth liners and goaltenders, and he made them believe that every day was indeed "a great day for hockey." Those weren't just words; they were his mantra, and everyone bought in as the playoffs began.

Every team is defined by something in the playoffs. Unfortunately for the Penguins, one of their constants was losing the opening game of each round that season. But each matchup also had its memorable moments. Against New Jersey, it was "The Save," a spectacular stop by backup goaltender Frank Pietrangelo versus Peter Stastny on the road. Only two days later, on home ice, Pietrangelo closed out the seven-game battle with a 4–0 shutout.

In the second round against the Washington Capitals, again after losing Game 1, Pens fans at the Arena were treated to a 7–6 overtime victory in which Stevens and Recchi finished with two goals each.

Although their first Cup victory was still two series away, the drama came in the third round against the Boston Bruins. After the team lost the first two in Boston by a combined score of 11–7, Stevens—a bold and brash Boston native—said the following to Dave Molinari, then of the *Pittsburgh Press*. "We're confident we can beat this team. And we will beat this team.... We'll beat this team. I'll say it right now, we'll beat them."

Armed with Stevens's confidence and his goal-scoring touch, the Penguins returned home to win the next four games, clinching at the Civic Arena with a 5–3 win. Stevens literally dominated his hometown team with 6 goals and 4 assists. In fact, in Game 3, following his prediction, Stevens opened the scoring at home as the Pens went on to a 4–1 victory.

Every series had a highlight, a showstopper, a turning point, but none of them had what Lemieux would do in Game 2 at the Civic Arena in the finals against the Minnesota North Stars. He scored what many believe is the signature goal of his career. When it was nominated for the title of "NHL's Greatest Moment" in a fan poll celebrating the League's one-hundredth anniversary in 2017, Phil Bourque—a talented blue-collar winger on Lemieux's line—had this to say to NHL.com: "Mario Lemieux used to yell a certain way when he wanted the puck, depending on how fast he wanted it. If you had time to pass, he would draw out the first syllable and say, 'Yee-ip.' If you didn't, he wouldn't. He'd say, 'Yip.' That meant, 'Get me the puck right away. It doesn't have to be on my tape,'" Bourque said.

In the second period of Game 2, the Pens were leading, 2–1. As Bourque came back in the defensive zone, he saw a rebound and said he heard "Yip" from Lemieux.

"I just threw it up in the same area code," Bourque said. "I knew if it was within four or five feet, he probably, with his reach, was going to get it. It was probably four feet behind him. He corralled it. I was making my way to the bench, and I witnessed maybe one of the greatest goals in NHL history (also from his interview on NHL.com)."

Just twenty-four hours apart in 1990, the Pirates began a series that would end their season and the Penguins began a season that would finish with a championship series. The Civic Arena faithful saw a perennial Stanley Cup champion being born.

11

DYNASTY UNFULFILLED

BY PAUL ALEXANDER

Everybody loves a winner. Everybody loves a parade. So, what's not to like about a Stanley Cup championship parade? After the 1993 Penguins closed the regular season as the NHL's best team, the two-time defending Stanley Cup champions certainly didn't need to meet with city officials to plan the parade route. They could use the same one they had used after the franchise's first two championships following the 1991 and 1992 seasons. Supposedly, there is no such thing as a sure thing. But this 1993 team was as close to being a lock for another Cup as Mario Lemieux was for hitting an empty net on a breakaway.

There's no way to diminish what the 1993 Pittsburgh Penguins accomplished during that historic regular season, especially when you factor in the obstacles they had to overcome along the way. The bumps in the road were more like venerable Pittsburgh potholes. The biggest one almost swallowed the Penguins and their entire season whole. The bomb that was dropped on January 12 registered a 9.5 on the Richter scale. Mario Lemieux stunned the hockey world with the news that he had Hodgkin's lymphoma. "Le Manifique" was on a record-setting points pace that was threatening to obliterate Wayne Gretzky's NHL record for goals and points in a season. "Super Mario" also had his Penguins poised to capture a third straight Stanley Cup.

Sadly, the disease and the aggressive radiation treatment left the superstar's career in jeopardy. Miraculously, he would miss only two months of action.

As if it were scripted, his return to the ice came in typical Lemieux fashion. March 2 was his last day of scheduled treatments, and he caught a flight to Philadelphia to join his teammates for a game against the Flyers in the Spectrum. Despite losing the game, 5–4, Super Mario tallied a goal and an assist. But the most memorable moment came when the infamous and notorious Philly faithful welcomed Mario with a standing ovation.

The comeback tour finally landed Lemieux on home ice at the Igloo against the Bruins on March 9. Mario contributed a helper in Pittsburgh's 3–2 win over the Bruins, but little did anyone know then that the Penguins and their captain were embarking on a historic run that may never be seen again.

Not even the twenty-five inches of snow that blanketed Pittsburgh on March 12 and 13 could slow down this juggernaut. Neither the Great Blizzard nor the mere mortals that represented the rest of the NHL were any match for this Penguin team.

On March 14, the Penguins edged the New York Islanders, 3–2, at the Nassau County Coliseum. The win was Pittsburgh's forty-second, and it gave the Pens their 90th point. Amazingly, with fifteen regular-season games left, these totals were new franchise highs, and Mario and his mates were just getting warmed up.

Lemieux's absence had allowed the rest of the league to believe the scoring race was actually up for grabs. Pat LaFontaine had the audacity to surpass the idle Lemieux by 12 points. There wasn't a whole lot of season left, but Mario wasn't shy about announcing that his intentions were to pass LaFontaine and anyone else who had their eye on his prize.

The wins and the goals just kept flowing like the cold beer and stiff drinks at Froggy's after the game. For Lemieux, 4- and 5-goal nights were pretty much routine. Remember that 12-point cushion LaFontaine enjoyed in the points race during Mario's absence? Kevin Stevens had called it, and Mario cruised to his fourth Art Ross Trophy with a 12-point cushion of his own.

The Penguins were like a runaway raft going over the falls. The wins were being stacked like pancakes at an all-you-can-eat breakfast. There was no question that the Presidents' Trophy for most points and that consecutive win streak were in the Pens' crosshairs. I'm sure that, in hindsight, those two feats would be traded like trinkets for Manhattan.

The 1992–93 Penguin team ended the regular season with an eye-popping 56-21-7-0 record. A Presidents' Trophy–worthy 119 points and an NHL-best 17-game winning streak still stand today. Their captain, playing in only 60 games, ran away with the Art Ross Trophy with 160 points (69 goals and 91 assists).

Before the 2005–6 season, the Penguins were struggling to rebuild their once-proud franchise. Thanks to the luck of the bounce in the 2005 NHL Draft lottery, they received the first pick in the draft and used it to choose one of the greatest talents the game has known, Sidney Crosby (87). Crosby has led the Pens to three Stanley Cup Championships while scoring 1,325 points as of 2020. *Courtesy of David Finoli.*

This was a team of destiny. This was a two-time defending Stanley Cup champion with superstars and dynasty written all over it. The record-setting winning streak certainly put the rest of the NHL on notice that another Cup was all but inevitable. During that seventeen-game winning streak, Le Manifique scored 27 goals and added 23 assists. All that was left now was the formality of the playoffs.

The Penguins were battle-tested and Stanley Cup warriors. After the tragic loss of Badger Bob Johnson, the legendary Scotty Bowman had stepped in, and the Penguins didn't skip a beat. The core of Mario Lemieux, Ron Francis, Kevin Stevens and the emerging Jaromir Jagr was more than formidable. General Manager Craig Patrick's masterful additions of Rick Tocchet and Kjell Sanmuelsson secured back-to-back Cups, and that iconic trophy was now a certainty for another dip in Mario's pool.

First up was the New Jersey Devils. After Pittsburgh cruised to an insurmountable three-games-to-none lead, the Devils extended the series to five games with a 4–1 win in Jersey. The Penguins matter-of-factly closed out the Devils, 5–3, at the Civic Arena. This dynasty-in-waiting was right on schedule.

As we all know, anything can happen in a seven-game series, but this was the Penguins and the New York Islanders. The Islanders had finished a ridiculous 32 points behind the Pens. New York did sneak by a well-rested Pittsburgh team, 3–2, in Game 1, but Tom Barrasso pitched a shutout in Game 2 as the Penguins evened the series with a 3–0 victory.

The Islanders weren't about to lie down, and with two wins apiece, it was still anyone's series. That was until Game 5. Mario Lemieux, Rick Tocchet and Larry Murphy all scored unanswered first-period goals, and the Penguins cruised to a 6–3 win. Sure, it has always been first to four, but this was Mario Lemieux and the Pittsburgh Penguins.

Game 6 was a shootout, and when it was all said and done, Uwe Krupp's empty-net goal iced it for the Isles and forced a Game 7. No worries. It was home ice and a Game 7 certainty for the Penguins.

As far as bad omens go, the Penguins experienced one of the absolutely most horrific ever. With no score less than three minutes into the game, 50-goal scorer Kevin Stevens collided with Rich Pilon in the corner. The collision was so vicious that Stevens was knocked out cold and landed face-first on the ice without even softening the blow with his arms.

Stevens smashed his nose and broke almost every bone in his face. The surgeons had to peel down his face from ear to ear, insert five metal plates and then close him up with one hundred stiches. Before any of that, the mostly coherent power forward listened to the end of the game on the radio.

While not nearly as devastating as the injury, hearing the call of David Volek's overtime game-winner was every bit as painful. This dynastic Penguin juggernaut that had just rewritten the franchise record book during the regular season would now be forever known as the best team not to win a championship. It truly is a flawed premise, but if you need perspective or a little understanding, ask any of the 1976 Steelers what that actually means.

12

THE LEMIEUX HAT TRICK

BY PAUL ALEXANDER

With forty career hat tricks and three more during the playoffs, Mario Lemieux sits at number two all-time in games in which he scored three or more goals. That's ten shy of the Great One, Wayne Gretzky. However, like the legendary Gordie Howe, Lemieux has his own triumvirate of accomplishments that constitute a "Lemieux Hat Trick." The "Howe Hat Trick" is scoring a goal, getting into a fight and adding an assist in the same game. Surprisingly, Howe achieved that only twice in a career that spanned parts of six decades. Lemieux's unique hat trick has accounted for five Stanley Cup championships and a burgeoning franchise with a very bright future.

So, what's the Lemieux Hat Trick? Unlike the traditional hockey version, his is more about saves than goals. It all started when the Penguins creatively found themselves with the worst record in the NHL. That moved them into position to select a truly generational talent with the first overall pick in the 1984 NHL draft. Let's call that the initial save. After scoring on his first shot of his first shift in an NHL game, Lemieux saved hockey in Pittsburgh by putting the Penguins on the map and eventually elevating the franchise into a Stanley Cup contender. He led the Cupless Penguins to back-to-back titles in 1991 and 1992. That is no small accomplishment when you consider how little interest and excitement the Penguins had generated since their inception in 1967.

The statue of Mario Lemieux breaking through two New Your Islander defensemen stands outside of the PPG Paints Arena. Arguably the greatest athlete to represent the city of Pittsburgh, Lemieux has been a pivotal part of all five Stanley Cup championships the franchise has secured, as both a player and an owner. *Courtesy of David Finoli.*

After an amazing career that had been sabotaged by cancer and two back surgeries, Lemieux was forced to save the Penguins again. He had retired the first time in 1997, and by 1999, his beloved Penguins were in bankruptcy and the owner, Roger Marino, owed Mario $31 million in deferred payments. Of course, Lemieux wanted his money. It was his. He had earned it. He also wanted to keep the Penguins in Pittsburgh. Marino, meanwhile, had requested permission to shop the franchise to other cities. That left the retired Hall of Famer one recourse. Lemieux had to find a way to buy the team.

None of this was going to be easy. Lemieux had his money guy, but the NHL had plenty of questions. At thirty-three, what's to keep one of the all-time great players from making a comeback? They watched John Spano go from the savior of the Islanders to a convicted felon behind bars. Bruce McNall, who brought Gretzky to Los Angeles, also went to jail for financial fraud. This was far from an empty net for Lemieux to fill up. In fact, the odds were stacked against the Lemieux group and the future of NHL hockey in Pittsburgh.

One of Lemieux's attorneys, Chuck Greenburg, brilliantly pointed out that with Lemieux as an owner, the franchise would see a huge jump in goodwill. This would rally the fans, jump-start the process to secure a new arena and significantly increase the value of the team. Lemieux had given the Penguins and their fans all he had for twelve years, and all he had to show for it was an "I owe you" for $31 million that probably wasn't worth the paper it was printed on.

Real money is exactly what the Lemieux Group needed to convince the NHL that it was a solvent and serious ownership group. Once the money man was vetted, the Lemieux Group was on the power play. With Lemieux in the high slot, Penguin fans were soon smiling like a butcher's dog.

Ron Burkle, who had gone from grocery store box boy to billionaire, was stepping in and stepping up to help his friend secure ownership of the franchise. From that moment in 1999 that brought Pittsburgh out of bankruptcy, Burkle has ensured that the Penguins organization wanted for nothing. Sure, there is a mandated salary cap for the players, but there are no limits on spending for facilities, front office staff and anything else that would give Pittsburgh an edge. All was well with the Pittsburgh Penguins. Or was it?

Despite two Stanley Cup championships, a lifetime of highlight-reel goals and saving the franchise from bankruptcy, Mario Lemieux still hadn't done enough to secure the Penguins' future in Pittsburgh. With the money already allocated for the new ballparks and stadiums for the commonwealth's professional football and baseball teams, the Penguins were looking at a hand slap instead of a handout.

No one in their right mind would ever question Lemieux's greatness as a player, but what none of us really knew about Mario was that he was also a superstar in the boardroom. When promises weren't kept and it looked like the new arena wasn't going to happen, Lemieux played hardball and said the Penguins were actively pursuing relocation. Kansas City just happened to have a brand-new arena and a sweetheart of a deal that was almost too good to pass up. Governor Ed Rendell, a seasoned politician, had met his match when Lemieux was across from him at the bargaining table.

In March 2007, a deal was consummated for a new arena, and once again, number 66 had made the Pittsburgh Penguins his top priority. With some creative financing that included the gaming licensee anteing up millions per year to pay down the debt of the arena, the Penguins were once again poised for greatness.

Let's just imagine that Mario Lemieux helped the Penguins win two Stanley Cups and didn't even make his amazing comeback. Sure, hockey wouldn't still be in Pittsburgh, but what about those memories? Or, what if he did save the franchise from bankruptcy in 1999 and we got to watch Sidney, Geno and the Flower win Cups at Spirit Arena in Kansas City? Everyone would still believe Mario did all he could, and the politicians would have been the villains.

Thankfully, the Lemieux Hat Trick has allowed for three more Stanley Cup championships and a franchise that any city would be proud to support. Maybe another individual or a player has done more for a franchise, but that is simply impossible to imagine.

13

SAYING GOODBYE

THE PENS' FINAL SEASON AT THE IGLOO

BY JOHN W. FRANKO

The Pittsburgh Penguins opened their 2009–10 campaign 112 days after their thrilling 2–1 win over the Red Wings in Game 7 of the Stanley Cup Finals.

A standing-room-only crowd of 17,132 marked the 119th consecutive sellout at Mellon Arena. It roared when the Penguins raised the banner commemorating the franchise's third Stanley Cup championship. It followed a twenty-five-minute ceremony. Video highlights rolled atop the arena's dome.

But the ceremony celebrated more than just another championship. It marked the Penguins' forty-third—and final—home opener at the igloo.

Brooks Orpik would later say that it was his favorite memory of the building. "When I got here we were with Washington and Chicago at the bottom of the barrel, so I really appreciate more than some of the younger guys having gone from the lowest of lows to the highest of highs," he said.

The Pens knocked off the Rangers, 3–2, and it was the beginning of a red-hot streak that saw the Pens win nine of their first ten games. They won their first four road games, setting a team record for road wins to start the season. They closed out October with a record of eleven wins and three losses and 22 points.

They opened November with a 4–3 win over Anaheim, but they began to cool off. They would lose five of their next seven, but they rebounded and were 19-9 after a 5–2 win over the Rangers on November 30. They would finish the first half of the season at 26-14-1.

With a young, talented team on the ice for the Pittsburgh Penguins, management chose a no-nonsense coach by the name of Michel Therrien to lead the team midway in the 2005–06 campaign. He led them to two playoff appearances the following two seasons that included an Eastern Conference Championship in 2008. *Courtesy of David Finoli.*

The Pens had a record of 36-22-4 when the season took a break for the 2010 Winter Olympics in Vancouver. Five players represented the team at the games—Orpik for the United States; Evgeni Malkin and Sergei Gonchar for Russia; and Sidney Crosby and Marc-Andre Fleury for Canada.

When the regular schedule resumed at the beginning of March, the Pens opened with a four-game winning streak. They finished the month 8-4-2.

They won three of their final five games to finish the regular season with a record of 47-28-7 and 101 points. More than fifty former Penguins, including Hall of Famers Mario Lemieux, Paul Coffey, Bryan Trottier, Craig Patrick, Larry Murphy and Andy Bathgate were on hand for a ceremony before the final regular-season home game on April 8.

The Penguins finished second in the Atlantic Division behind New Jersey and were the fourth seed in the Eastern Conference. The Washington Capitals finished first in the Eastern Conference and clinched home ice throughout the playoffs, but Caps coach Bruce Boudreau said that as reigning champions, the Pens were "the team to beat in the upcoming tournament."

The Pens opened the Eastern Conference quarterfinals on April 14 at home against Ottawa. Malkin found the net twice, and Craig Adams and Alex Goligoski added single tallies, but the Senators came away with a 5–4 win.

Pittsburgh fell behind early in Game 2, but Crosby tied it midway through the first period, and Kris Letang netted the game-winner with less than four minutes left in regulation.

Game 3 in Ottawa was tied at one midway through the second period when Malkin and Crosby both scored to give the Pens a two-goal lead at the intermission. Bill Guerin scored in the third on the way to a 4–2 win and a 2-1 series lead.

In Game 4, Malkin gave the Pens a first-period lead. Two goals by Crosby and another by Matt Cooke within a twenty-five-second span gave them a 4–0 lead. Senator goaltender Brian Elliott went to the bench and was replaced by Pascal Leclaire.

The Senators would cut the deficit to two, but Maxime Talbot, Kris Kunitz and Jordan Staal scored on the way to a 7–4 victory.

With a chance to wrap up the series at home, the Pens saw the Senators jump to a 2–0 first-period lead. But two goals by Kunitz and another by Crosby gave them a 3–2 advantage midway through the third. The Senators quickly tied it, however, and the teams battled it out for almost sixty more minutes before Matt Carkner's goal at 7:06 of the third overtime gave the Senators a 4–3 win.

The Senators looked like they were ready to even the series when they jumped out to a 3–0 lead midway through the second period in Game 6 in Ottawa. A goal by Cooke gave the Pens life, and they entered the third period down 3–1. Guerin scored on a power play seven minutes into the period, and Cooke scored his second goal five minutes later to tie it.

The game went into overtime, and both teams had great opportunities to win it. Paschal Dupuis notched the game-winner on an assist from Staal at 9:56.

The Pens were heavy favorites when they faced the eighth-seed Montreal Canadiens in the Eastern Conference Semifinals. The Canadiens had upset top-seeded Washington in the first round.

The Pens handled Montreal in a 6–3 home win in Game 1. Gonchar, Staal, Letang, Adams, Goligoski and Guerin all tallied in the victory. But hopes for a quick series were dashed when Montreal came back with a 3–1 win two days later.

Behind goals from Malkin and Dupuis, the Pens retook the series lead with a 2–0 win in Montreal in Game 3. In Game 4, Talbot and Kunitz found

Ron Scuderi was a solid defenseman for the Pittsburgh Penguins in the early part of the twenty-first century. In 2009, he made a clutch stop in Game 6 of the Stanley Cup Finals off a shot by Detroit's Johan Franzen with a wide-open net behind him to help preserve a 2–1 win, allowing the Pens to capture the Cup a game later in Detroit. *Courtesy of Boston College Athletics.*

the back of the net, but the pesky Canadiens once again evened the series with a 3–2 win.

Back in Pittsburgh, goals by Letang and Gonchar gave the Pens a 2–1 win and a 3–2 lead in the series. But Montreal responded with a 4–3 win at home, and the series went back to Pittsburgh for the decisive Game 7.

It was ugly. Crosby took a penalty just ten seconds into the game, and Montreal took the lead on the ensuing power play twenty-two seconds later. Another goal at the 14:23 mark gave them a 2–0 lead at the first intermission.

Two more goals—including a short-handed tally—in the first 5:14 of the second period increased Montreal's lead to 4–0. Goals by Kunitz at 8:36 and Staal at 16:30 gave the Pens hope heading into the third, but a power play goal by Brian Gionta at the 10:00 mark put the game away for the Canadiens.

With the season over, the players and staff prepared to say goodbye to their old home.

"When I got here I found out pretty quickly that this arena has an amazing feel," Crosby said. "It's an atmosphere you have to be at to describe. The crowd feels like it is on top of you, they are so involved in the game."

"It might be the oldest building in the league but we have everything we need," added Orpik. "It might be old wood and it might smell old, and it might not be that pretty, but it's a great building to play in."

Coach Dan Bylsma summed it up when he said: "Walking out of the tunnel with two minutes until the start of a playoff game with a white-out and the fans going 'Let's go Pens' is something I will never forget either, and will miss that about this building."

14

GOING OUT ON TOP

THE HORNETS SAY GOODBYE WITH A CALDER CUP

BY JOHN W. FRANKO

When Billy Harris whipped home a rebound twenty-six seconds into overtime on April 30, 1967, the Pittsburgh Hornets captured their third American Hockey League Calder Cup in their final home game ever.

The win gave the Hornets a four-game sweep over the Rochester Americans. They had tied the game with less than thirty seconds left in regulation on a goal by Terry Gray.

With the new NHL franchise Pittsburgh Penguins becoming new tenants of the Civic Arena that fall, there would be no place for the Hornets.

"It took a lot of doing in the final 61 seconds of their existence in Pittsburgh, but the Hornets closed out 26 seasons of hockey in this city last night by winning their third Calder Cup," wrote the *Post-Gazette*'s Jimmy Jordan the following day.

A headline in the *Pittsburgh Press* said simply, "The Hornets Leave 'Em Laughing."

An affiliate of the Detroit Red Wings, the Hornets had finished the 1966–67 regular season first in the West Division with 92 points, 7 ahead of the Americans. They were third in scoring with 282 goals and first in goals against, allowing just 209.

As an affiliate, the Hornets were part of a Detroit-Memphis-Pittsburgh "shuttle service" that saw players moving throughout the year, but they had still become a close-knit unit.

The Hershey Bears won the East Division and were the Hornets' opponent in the first round of the AHL playoffs. The Hornets took the series, 4–1, but the first four games were tight, with the Hornets winning 4–2, 3–2 and 3–2 before the Bears kept the series alive with a 3–1 win.

The Hornets closed out the series with a 4–0 win in Pittsburgh.

Rochester, meanwhile, survived a tough five-game series against the Cleveland Barons, winning it, 3–2. They came back from a 2–0 deficit.

While the quirky playoff format forced the Hornets to win four games instead of three in the first round, it gave them a second-round bye. The Americans had to face off against the Baltimore Clippers. They took the series, 3–1, but several players were injured. Combined with the tough opening round, they would enter the finals a tired team.

The opening game of the series was scheduled to be at Rochester, but a women's bowling tournament forced it to be moved to Pittsburgh on April 26.

Hornet manager-coach Baz Bastien wondered if his team would be sluggish after an eleven-day layoff, but goals by Ted Taylor, Gary Garrett and Gray within a four-minute span midway through the first period put his fears to rest. Val Fonteyne added two unassisted goals—the second short-handed—and the Hornets win on to win, 7–1.

The thirty-one-year-old Fonteyne had carved out an NHL career as a penalty killer. "I've been doing it for so long, I consider it a challenge," said the center, who at 155 pounds was the lightest player on the team. "I don't mind it at all. That's what kept me in the NHL."

The series moved back to Rochester for Game 2. Bastien was confident that one road win would be enough for the Hornets to capture the title. "If we were to win this one, I think they'd throw in the sponge," said the normally cautious manager-coach. "We haven't won here all year, but we've played well."

Upset by losing the first game because of the scheduling conflict, Rochester fans circulated a petition inside the War Memorial Auditorium. It protested the treatment of the team by the commission running the auditorium.

The Americans rewarded the standing-room-only crowd of 7,683 with an inspired performance. The Hornets opened the scoring with a goal by Dan McKenney in the first period, but the Amerks tied it before intermission.

Taylor gave the Hornets the lead again on a power play goal midway through the second period. The goal would stand up as the Hornets survived a furious onslaught by the Amerks in the final period. Goaltender Hank Bassen made a number of outstanding saves, and the Hornets held on for a 2–1 win.

Bob Johnson played hockey for the University of Minnesota Golden Gophers. He eventually became a successful collegiate and professional coach before coming to Pittsburgh in 1990. His positive attitude was a key factor in the Penguins capturing their first Stanley Cup that year. Sadly, he developed brain cancer and died in November 1991. *Courtesy of the University of Minnesota Athletics.*

The tough loss seemed to take the fight out of the Americans, and they looked tired in Game 3 in Pittsburgh. The Hornets controlled the game from the outset and won, 5–1, setting the stage for a sweep the following night.

But it wouldn't be easy. With the champagne already on ice, the Hornets found themselves down 2–0 early in the third period. Captain Ab McDonald tied it with goals nineteen seconds apart, but the Amerks retook the lead midway through the period.

They still held the lead with just over a minute to go in regulation, when Bastien pulled Bassen in favor of a sixth attacker. With thirty-five seconds to go, Bobby Wall won a faceoff and sent the puck to McKenney, who fired a hard shot off goaltender Bobby Perrault. Gray found the rebound in the wild scramble that followed and fired a shot over the fallen Perrault to tie it.

The crowd barely had time to settle into their seats for the overtime before the game was over. Following the faceoff, Jarrett rushed into the Rochester zone and fired a shot off Perrault. Harris was there to flip the rebound over him, and a wild celebration erupted.

Wall barely missed a serious injury when a teammate's stick struck him in the eye as he jumped over the boards from the team bench to join in. "We came from two goals behind, it takes a champion to do that," he said later.

Bastien was pacing behind the bench, and he admitted that he missed the goal. "I didn't see it," he said. "I heard the crowd yell and couldn't believe it."

A jubilant McDonald had a practical reason for wanting the series to end as soon as possible. "You don't get paid for playing any more games," he said.

Jarrett was also happy, because now he would be able to begin business classes at Ryerson Polytechnic Institute in Toronto the next day.

The only negative for the Hornets during their playoff run was the attendance. They drew a total of 31,684 for their six home dates, with a crowd of 5,169 for the Cup-clincher.

A farewell party for the players was hosted by the Hornets' booster club at the North Side Elks. "I'd like to coach this bunch again," Bastien said after the party. "They were fun to work with. They really went out and played for you, and were best when it was toughest, like Sunday night."

The players were the property of the Red Wings, and a number were selected in the expansion player draft. McDonald and Fonteyne were selected by the Penguins. Harris was selected by the California Golden Seals, Gray by the Los Angeles Kings, Taylor by the Minnesota North Stars and McKenney by the St. Louis Blues.

15

THE SUMMIT AT CENTER ICE

THE RUSSIANS COME TO PITTSBURGH

BY GARY KINN

In late December 1975, times overall were fairly good for the city of
Pittsburgh and for sports fans in the Steel City. Headlines in the *Pittsburgh
Press* on Sunday, December 28, 1975, indicated that the city's core business
of steel production was expected to be at increased levels in 1976. Pittsburgh
saw perhaps one of the most dominant and best single-season pro football
teams ever assembled pound the Baltimore Colts at five-year-old Three
Rivers Stadium, 28–10, in the first round on the NFL playoffs. But the
entire world of hockey, including Pittsburgh, did not share the same level of
optimism heading into 1976.

Just three years earlier, in September 1972, a team of Canadian all-
stars had struggled mightily against a team from the Soviet Union, known
appropriately as the Red Army, in an international hockey series known as
the Summit Series. The Canadian club assembled for the Summit Series
featured all-time great players such as Phil Esposito, Bobby Clarke, Brad
Park and future Hall of Fame goaltenders Ken Dryden and Tony Esposito
on its roster. The Canadian team was so deep in talent that future Hall of
Fame entrant Marcel Dionne never played a single minute in the series.
Vic Hadfield, a 1975–76 Pittsburgh Penguin forward, was on the Summit
Series roster in 1972.

The majority of hockey press in Canada seemed to be in universal
agreement that the Canadian all-star team would likely win every game in
the series. The Soviets were repeatedly expected to struggle with the rigors

The Pittsburgh Penguins' Ryan Malone (12) and Evgeni Malkin (71) get into a scuffle with the Philadelphia Flyers during a game at the Civic Arena. Malkin has become one of the greatest Penguins in the franchise's history. He won the Calder Trophy as Rookie of the Year as well as the Conn Smyth as the 2009 Stanley Cup playoff MVP in leading the team to their third championship. *Courtesy of David Finoli.*

of the straight-ahead, body-checking, far more physical North American style of play. In Game 1 of the series on September 2, 1972, at the venerable Montreal Forum, the pundits appeared to be correct for all of ten minutes of action. Phil Esposito scored on Canada's first shift just thirty seconds into the contest, and forward Paul Henderson scored six minutes later. The hockey world appeared to settle in for the rout of the Soviets in the series. But it was not meant to be. The Red Army scored two quick goals in the second half of the first period to end the period tied, 2–2. More disturbing was the fact that the bigger, more structured Canadians simply could not keep up with the speedy, circling, synchronized and well-conditioned Russians on nearly every shift. The differences between the two styles of play became even more pronounced in the second period, as the Red Army potted the only two goals on the way to an eventual runaway 7–3 victory. In a single night and contest, the Russian Red Army club had demonstrated a playing style and philosophy that would ultimately start a process to a changed world of pro and amateur hockey. The Summit Series did develop into a tense eight-game series, finally won by Canada four wins to three (one tie) on a very late goal in Game 8. But the stellar play of the Russians put the NHL on notice and caused significant concern throughout North American pro hockey about playing the Russians again head-to-head.

In addition to questions arising about style and philosophy of play in North America after the Summit Series, both the NHL and the fledgling World Hockey Association had also been struggling with a public image of excessive violence and rough play in 1975. Numerous fights occurred in many games, including a number of incidents each season of bench-emptying brawls. The Philadelphia Flyers, a far better offensive and defensive team than the reputation that they carried, did win back-to-back Stanley Cups in 1974 and 1975, all while leading the NHL in fighting majors and overall penalty minutes and using outright physical intimidation of opponents.

Against this backdrop, the NHL did agree to play a series of exhibition games between two of the top Soviet clubs from the Soviet Championship League and NHL opponents, to be known as the Super Series '76. Soviet teams had never played against NHL league teams up to this point. A series of eight exhibition games was scheduled for late December 1975 through mid-January 1976. The Soviets sent their top two clubs to America and Canada, the Red Army club and their Soviet Wings club. The Soviets were confident enough that they agreed to schedule games against the current NHL champion Flyers and the eventual 1975–76 Stanley Cup champs Montreal Canadiens. The second game of the series was scheduled to take place on Monday, December 29, at the Civic Arena in Pittsburgh against the Penguins.

Once again, it became clear from the beginning of the announced Super Series that the Soviets did not see the games as exhibitions. The Red Army brought future Hall of Fame netminder Vladislav Tretiak with them for the four scheduled Red Army games. Tretiak was a pioneer in numerous areas of goaltending philosophy, with many of his techniques and style utilized in the NHL to this day. In Pittsburgh, the Soviet Wings coaching staff arrived to watch and scout the Penguins a week early in a game against the Atlanta Flames to prepare for their opener with the team. The Wings added future Hall of Fame forward Alexander Yakushev, one of the best players for the Soviets in the Summit Series in 1972, to the Soviet Wings roster for the club's scheduled games. Current Penguin Hadfield repeated often to the press

In 1975, when the Soviets came to the Civic Arena to face the Penguins, seeing a player from Russia in an NHL uniform was nonexistent. By the twenty-first century, they were an integral part of just about every team in the league. Shown here is Sergei Gonchar (55), among the best who ever played the game. By the time he retired, he had scored more goals and points than any other Russian defenseman in NHL history. *Courtesy of David Finoli.*

that the conditioning and practice habits of the Soviets should make North American clubs wary. In the first game of the Super Series, the Red Army routed the New York Rangers, 7–3, with Tretiak in goal. Ranger forward Steve Vickers commented to the press that the Rangers might not be able to beat the Soviets on the New York team's best night.

The 1975–76 Penguins were a fairly competitive team in their own right. The team went 35-33-12 and made the playoffs after the regular season. Although the Pens were eliminated in the first round by the Toronto Maple Leafs, the club featured two 50-plus goal scorers and 100-plus-point forwards in Pierre Larouche and Jean Pronovost, as well as a 99-point season by fan favorite Syl Apps. A young Rick Kehoe contributed 29 goals, while J. Bob

"Battleship" Kelly, Colin Campbell and Steve Durbano kept the peace on the ice. Former number-one pick in the 1968 NHL draft, Michel Plasse, had perhaps his best overall pro season in 1975-76 in the Pittsburgh goal.

At 7:30 p.m. on Monday, December 29, 1975, the puck dropped at the Civic Arena between the Soviet Wings club and the Penguins in the second game of the eight-game Summit Series. For the 13,218 in attendance that night, likely unaware at that time that they were watching a game significant in hockey history, the end result was clearly a disappointment. The Wings tallied 2 goals in the first 4:33 of the first period, then scored 2 more over the next ten minutes of the first period to end the frame at 4–0. The Wings went up 5–0 before the Pens made it respectable with 3 second-period scores in a 7–4 loss with Plasse in the net. Pens defensemen Dave Burrows and Hadfield indicated that the team likely got caught standing and watching the speedy, flowing Soviets too much early in the contest. But the two Soviet clubs ended the Super Series '76 with a combined five wins, two losses and one tie. Their success in North America eventually opened doors to numerous players from Eastern Europe to enter the NHL and to truly start the process to globalize pro hockey.

III

MUSIC

16

THE BOSS

BRUCE SPRINGSTEEN MAKES HIS IMPACT ON THE CIVIC ARENA

By Lance Jones

I was a senior in college the first time I saw Bruce Springsteen live. It was on February 19, 1975 at Penn State in the 2,600-capacity University Auditorium on campus, and this show literally changed my life. It was inspirational in both length and substance, practically converting the crowd from "audience" into "congregation," for we'd been zapped, entranced and bound together through some sort of E Street electricity. It transformed me into a lifelong worshipper of "The Boss."

The very next night he played the Syria Mosque in Pittsburgh, and this marathon spectacle essentially jump-started the city's long love affair with Bruce Springsteen & the E Street Band. Bruce returned to the Mosque in August 1975 and April 1976, played at St. Vincent's College in 1977 and then easily mustered doubleheaders at the Stanley Theatre in August and December 1978.

Bruce's next concerts in Pittsburgh were on November 30 and December 1, 1980, at the Civic Arena in support of his new album, *The River*. The cult of Bruce had grown over the previous handful of years to such a degree that the true believers were now being joined in far greater numbers by new converts. It seemed that *everybody* had a hungry heart.

I was there the first night. Bruce and his band seemed to adapt instantaneously to this new, larger environment, and before the first song ended, he had absolute command over this crowd that was easily four

Looking through the crowd during his 1980 tour is the legendary Bruce Springsteen. Springsteen would be one of the main attractions during the fifty-year existence of the Civic Arena. *Courtesy of Tom Aikens.*

times the size of the ones at the Stanley Theatre. There was something magical happening. The entire audience began simply flat-out *roaring* after certain songs. And at times I found myself throatily hooting along until the tingle at the base of my neck skittered up like a mushroom cloud through the back of my head.

I had felt this way before, of course, from my college experience and then from seeing Springsteen later on in Pittsburgh at the Mosque and the Stanley. Things were certainly amped up now with Bruce's ascension to arena level in terms of crowd size, but once again I quickly came to believe that all of us were in some kind of communal grip, connected as one.

Bruce and the band had come to conquer. That night (and the next) they proved themselves to be eternally committed caretakers of rock's eternal flame, pumping out a staggering thirty-plus songs over two sets, including an encore that was more than eleven minutes long, a joyous excursion through classics including "Devil with a Blue Dress On / Good Golly Miss Molly," "C.C. Rider / Jenny Take a Ride" and a "I Hear a Train" interlude—part song, part exhortation—that sought to have the entire audience climb aboard Bruce and the band's blistering rock 'n' roll express.

Bruce and his band went on to play the Civic Arena nine more times before the wrecking ball took down the venue in September 2011 to make way for the Penguins' new arena: September 21 and 22, 1984 (the Born in the U.S.A. tour); March 20, 1988 (the Tunnel of Love Express tour); December 16, 1992 (the 1992–'93 world tour); April 25 and 26, 2000 (the 1999–2000 Reunion tour); December 4, 2002, as part of The Rising tour (the Civic Arena, now called Mellon Arena); November 14, 2007 (the Magic tour); and May 19, 2009 (the Working on a Dream tour).

I recently reached out to a few prominent Pittsburghers who were always close to the action when Bruce came to town. What follows are their remembrances.

RICH ENGLER, BOOKER OF Bruce's Pittsburgh concerts for DiCesare-Engler Productions:

In 1999, when Bruce and the E Street Band reunited after a decade apart, I received a call from his agent, Barry Bell, who said that Bruce was itching to get out and play. I called the arena and put April 25 and 26, 2000, on hold. We put the first show on sale, and it immediately sold out, so we quickly added the second show—gone! When Springsteen plays, he gives every ounce of his energy from beginning to end, performing like it's his very first concert—or his last! Both of these shows were sold 360 degrees, so over the two nights there were almost 34,000 fans in attendance.

Ed Traversari, marketer and handler of artist settlements for DiCesare-Engler:

I have so many memories of doing Springsteen shows in Pittsburgh, but unfortunately it was always hard for me to get to watch them since we were always working during these concerts. At one of the Civic Arena shows, Bruce's tour accountant and I were sitting in the backstage area figuring out how much Bruce was going to make that night. Down the hall I heard the beginning of "Jungleland"—a tune I love!—so I asked the tour accountant if there was any way that we could put the settlement on hold for a few minutes so I could go out and watch this one song. He agreed, so I left to go watch "Jungleland" from the side of the stage. When it was over I went back to reconnect with the band's tour accountant, and we finished our work. That was a special night—and I don't think I ever asked a favor like that from any other band through the years!

On November 30 and December 1, 1980, Bruce Springsteen made his first appearances at the Civic Arena. It was a graduation to major arenas after a career of playing colleges and smaller venues to that point. Springsteen was promoting his new album, *The River*, on those evenings, to the delight of the sellout crowds. *Courtesy of Tom Aikens.*

Joe Grushecky, Pittsburgh musician and decades-long friend of Bruce's who joined him onstage a total of seven times at the Pittsburgh Civic Arena; his first cameo appearance there with Bruce was in 1988:

> *The first show I ever saw at the arena was the Dave Clark Five on June 4, 1964. Going to Pittsburgh from my hometown of Biddle way out in Westmoreland County in those days was a major undertaking. The Burgh was considered to be a far-off strange land, but my buddy's older brother managed to drive us right to the entrance without once getting lost. The band that night blew me away. I was so excited that a while later, I somehow convinced my mom and dad to drive me back there to see the Stones in 1965. "Okay," they said, "but you have to take your younger brother, and don't lose him." No problem. I won't let him out of my sight. When the Stones hit with "Not Fade Away," I promptly abandoned him in the cheap seats to rush the stage and managed to get close enough to feel*

the bass pounding in my chest. Much to my relief, after I calmed down from my rock-and-roll contact high, the little guy was waiting patiently where I had left him!

Flash-forward to March 20, 1988. I anxiously wait at the side of the stage to join Bruce Springsteen and the mighty E Street Band for a guest appearance playing "Raise Your Hand" by Mr. Eddie Floyd. At the Civic Freakin' Arena! On the same stage that had given me so many thrills sitting in the audience. I had played there once before when our band opened for The Outlaws, but this time felt different. Bruce introduces me, and I step on that stage. Max counts to four and the band kicks in, and there I am riding the wave with one of the world's greatest rock bands.

17

THE FABS AND THE KING

ROCK'S HIGHEST ROYALTY GRACED THE ARENA
WITH THEIR PRESENCE—IF I HAD ONLY BEEN THERE

BY CHRIS FLETCHER

Sometimes we forget the building's origin as a concert venue. Civic Light Opera. Civic Arena. Makes sense. Acoustics be damned.

For me, the Igloo, as it came to be known for its domed shape and its hosting of the Pittsburgh Penguins, was a sports facility first and foremost. This was despite having seen a few concerts there, starting with my first real show, KISS, as a teen. I was also there for Bruce Springsteen, U2, Bob Seger, the Grateful Dead, the Go-Go's and a few other performances. I am fortunate enough to have twice experienced the midconcert opening of the Arena roof, a monumental and expensive engineering feat.

But I also think about the shows I didn't see there, even though my snobby musical tastes seldom land in the genre of large-venue concerts. (The Jam, the Style Council or solo Paul Weller took the stage at the Arena.) Sure, it would have been nice to catch Humble Pie with Steve Marriott (the best blue-eyed soul singer ever). The review in the *Pittsburgh Press* said Marriott brought the "worst display of vulgar language in Pittsburgh's rock history." Thirty days in the hole, indeed. But the two acts I would have wanted most to see live at the Arena were the two biggest in rock history—the Beatles and Elvis Presley. Yes, I was not even three when the Beatles played in 1964, and I was about fourteen and listening mostly to the Fab Four when the King played in 1976. But with time travel, all things are possible.

These were two acts that were interrelated. What if an American sailor hadn't landed in Liverpool with a copy of the King's debut album, the one with the Elvis Presley name printed in pink and green in a right angle next to the image of the young rocker with his acoustic guitar? It's said that even before he listened to the raw and exciting mix of country and blues, John Lennon saw the album cover and knew he wanted to be a rock star. This despite the chiding from his aunt Mimi, who raised him after his mother's death. "A guitar's all right, John," she said, "but you'll never earn a living by it."

By 1964, Lennon and his mates were earning a record-setting living. The Beatles supplanted Presley as the top-selling act in the world, with the Fabs having the top five songs in the April *Billboard* 100 and seven other songs charting at the same time—a mind-boggling achievement.

On September 14, John, Paul, George and Ringo steamrolled into Pittsburgh. The Beatles in 1964 were still fresh-faced with matching suits. They tore through a twelve-song set in under forty minutes. They mixed potent original songs with covers of the Isley Brothers ("Twist and Shout," which would become *their* song), Chuck Berry ("Roll over Beethoven," with George handling vocals), the Shirelles ("Boys," a Ringo crowd-pleaser) and Little Richard ("Long Tall Sally," with Paul at his rocking best). Fans screamed in sheer delight at "All My Loving," the song that opened the band's appearance on *The Ed Sullivan Show*.

The road was grueling, but this was a band that had built its chops in Hamburg, Germany, and in the Cavern Club in Liverpool. But in Pittsburgh, like most dates on that initial American tour, the Beatles played before twelve-thousand-plus screaming kids who created a crowd noise that would have drowned out a jet engine. The band played without monitors and couldn't hear themselves performing. That they were able to play on the same beat gives credence to Ringo being one of, if not the best, drummer of all time.

Because of the technical limitations of the day and heavy touring schedule, they grew less satisfied with their performances. Two years later, a show at Candlestick Park would be their last major concert appearance, except for a short rooftop performance in '69. The Beatles would head to the studio and further disrupt rock music, but that came at a cost. A look at the Fab Four at the end of the decade would show the effects of years of wear and tear, the once fresh faces hidden behind grizzled beards.

The 1970s was also not initially kind to the King. Presley had gone from rock icon to movie actor to Vegas cabaret star. He had played the Arena in '73 to mixed reviews and was making a return appearance on New Year's Eve 1976. There he summoned up some of the old magic. One of Presley's strengths had always been his ability to interpret material, putting his unique

Michael Jackson came to the Pittsburgh Civic Arena for three shows between September 26 and 28, 1988. Shown here with the Arena's director of marketing, Ida D'Errico, Jackson was at the height of his popularity as he came to the city on the second American leg of his successful Bad Tour. *Courtesy of Ida D'Errico.*

spin on it. It started on that debut album with the first track, as he absolutely killed Carl Perkins's "Blue Suede Shoes." When you hear, "It's one for the money, two for the show," I challenge you not to think of Elvis. He included "Blue Suede Shoes" and another cover from that album, Ray Charles's "I Got a Woman," when he took the stage at the Arena shortly before midnight.

The King also paused to welcome in the New Year with a version of "Auld Lang Syne." From there, it was back to a blistering set, with Presley standards like "Hound Dog," "It's Now or Never," "Little Sister" (my personal fave of his) and "Can't Help Falling in Love." The King served notice that he was still a performer to be reckoned with. He even included some newer material from Gordon Lightfoot ("Early Morning Rain") and the Eagles ("Tryin' to Get to You").

But that drink from the fountain of youth was brief. In August 1977, a depressed, bloated Presley was found dead in his mansion, Graceland. Officially, his death was ruled a heart attack, but Elvis was a heavy user of a number of prescription medications, including opiates, barbiturates and sedatives. When the toxicology report of his blood came back from analysis several weeks after his death, it reportedly contained high dosages of, among other things, the opiates Dilaudid, Percodan and Demerol, as well as Quaaludes and codeine.

Lennon, for his part, remarked snidely, "Elvis died the minute he went into the U.S. Army." He claimed that it was taken out of context and deeply regretted that statement. Lennon would never play in Pittsburgh again, either. He was gunned down outside his apartment in New York City in 1980, news brought to much of the nation by Howard Cosell during a *Monday Night Football* broadcast.

Of the remaining Beatles, only McCartney and Starr would play in town again, but neither at the Arena. Macca helped open the building that replaced it. Ringo and his All-Starr Band would play gigs at smaller venues. Harrison's ill-fated Dark Horse tour never made it here before the singer lost his voice. Lung cancer took him in 2001.

There are the what-ifs. What if the Beatles had reunited and accepted the monster payday offered in the mid-1970s for a reunion tour? Even *Saturday Night Live* got into the act, with an on-air invitation to come and play. Strangely, McCartney was visiting Lennon in New York at the time, and they almost took a cab to the studio. What if Presley had taken care of himself and had been able to usher in the 1950s and '60s throwback tours that became so popular? Would either have made stops in Pittsburgh?

But on at least two dates, the Civic Arena hosted rock royalty of the highest echelon. People who saw the Fabs and the King can lay claim to witnessing two of the building's legendary musical nights. I only wish I had been there.

18

THE SKYLINE SERIES

BY LANCE JONES

Back in 1985, I joined the Pittsburgh Civic Arena, which had been looking for a director of booking to help the venue move more into self-promotion of concerts. The Civic Arena Corporation team that was already in place at my arrival was an entrepreneurial and talented crew of department heads and staff who'd been charged by arena-and-hockey-team owner Edward J. DeBartolo Sr. to bring in more events.

In the mid-1980s, it was a tad unusual for an arena to dive right into booking its own concerts; we may have been one of just a handful of similarly sized indoor venues across the country taking charge of its own destiny, not waiting by the phone for an outside promoter to bring in concert attractions.

The Civic Arena ended up doing a number of concerts between 1985 and 1990 as "in-house promoter," meaning that we, the venue, booked the shows directly for all risk and reward, handled the marketing and sponsorship and ultimately lived or died by the success or failure of each concert.

One of the most exciting and ultimately rewarding challenges for the Civic Arena team was mounting the Skyline Series, the subscription series of open-air concerts under the stars. Our arena was an engineering marvel, built in 1961 with a retractable stainless-steel roof that enabled—weather-permitting and via the touch of a button—our audience to suddenly experience an "outdoor show" in the heart of the Steel City.

During the mid-1980s, the arena's vice-president-of-marketing-turned-general-manager was Tom Rooney. He recalls the origin of the Skyline Series and cites as inspiration a trip to Chastain Park in Atlanta, Georgia, in 1986 for a meeting with concert promoter Alex Cooley. Cooley and company ran a summer concert subscription series at a *true* outdoor amphitheater (capacity six thousand), and part of the allure for its subscribers were the white-linen and candelabra-covered tables in front of the stage, where groups of six could party all night, enjoying their own princely packed picnic baskets of wine and cheese while taking in the sounds of their favorite artists.

Rooney recalls as well the *motive* for Civic Arena Corporation to develop its own version of Chastain Park's successful series; it was, he says, "the burgeoning amphitheater business." Across the country, outdoor concert facilities were springing up like monied mushrooms in the mid-to-late 1980s, and our proactive thought process in Pittsburgh led us to develop our *own* "amphitheater" to potentially forestall one coming along somewhere else within our market. And it was the Civic Arena's unique roof-opening capability that turned our strategic thinking into a reality.

For that inaugural year of 1987 and the two that followed, Miller Beer signed on as the title sponsor of our new subscription series, and our venue's VP of communications and sales, Bill Strong, handled all of these sponsorship logistics with the Gary M. Reynolds Company, Miller's advertising agency based in Milwaukee.

And so the Skyline Series came into being, and we gave our newborn what we hoped would be a nourishing formula:

- *We'd book around five or six shows each summer, concentrating on the more mass-appeal, middle-of-the-road artists.*
- *We'd sell these five or six shows as a series, offering up the white-linen tables (à la Chastain's formula) for a premium price on the floor of the venue. For the rest of the arena—that is, the "lovely" orange permanent fixed seats—we'd offer a more digestible price.*
- *We'd actively promote the fact that all of these shows would be "roof open, weather permitting!"*
- *Lastly, we'd open up the five or six shows to individual ticket sales after the pre-identified period of subscription series sales had ended.*

In the end—in terms of bottom-line success over a three-year span—the Skyline Series scored with some very solid at-bats, with only a few errant swings for the fences. On the fan side of the equation, the public really embraced the concept of watching their stars while under the stars. Civic Arena Corporation had produced a winner for the city of Pittsburgh.

SKYLINE SERIES CONCERTS
AT THE PITTSBURGH CIVIC ARENA, 1987–89

Artists who appeared as part of the Skyline Series included the Beach Boys on June 24, 1987; Dan Fogelberg and his band on July 8, 1987; the Moody Blues on July 16, 1987; The VH-1 Classic Superfest on July 28, 1987, starring Tommy James & the Shondells, with the Turtles, Herman's Hermits, Mark Lindsay of Paul Revere & the Raiders, the Grass Roots featuring Rob Grill and the Byrds; The Dirty Dancing Tour on June 29, 1988, starring Bill Medley along with Eric Carmen, the Contours and Merry Clayton; Chicago on July 27, 1988; James Taylor on July 30, 1988; Kenny Loggins on August 24, 1988; Hall & Oates on September 12, 1988; Jackson Browne on July 1, 1989; Bob Dylan on July 28, 1989; the Doobie Brothers on August 3, 1989; and a Woodstock-on-fumes reunion tour called "'69–'89: Twentieth Anniversary Celebration Tour," featuring Richie Havens, John Sebastian, Canned Heat and Buddy Miles with Ricky Hendrix (Jimi's a-bit-less-talented brother).

INTERESTING REACTIONS FROM
SOME OF THE PERFORMERS

- Tom Rooney remembers that Hall & Oates were surprised to find they were scheduled to play our side summer stage instead of the standard end-stage arena setup, in which the floor sections have all chairs and no white-linen tables. From the stage early in their performance, the duo told the audience that the "tables looked like 'Vegas on the Mon.'"
- When Dan Fogelberg was performing, the arena roof began to open up on schedule—and then it stopped due to an untimely electrical failure of the roof-opening process. It was stuck at three feet open, and a few folks in the increasingly restless and disappointed crowd began yelling "Open the roof!" during an especially tender Fogelberg ballad.
- Rooney remembers another occasion when the Civic Arena's roof was a bit problematic: "At the James Taylor concert we turned a potential disaster into something special when— after the first half of his set, with the roof closed due to wind

conditions and fans chanting 'Open it up!'—we *did* finally open the roof for his second set, alongside James's improvised version of 'Up on the Roof'. "

- Kenny Loggins had Tom Rooney and I summoned to see him backstage, where he voiced his displeasure at the table setup on the floor, saying that his true fans weren't at those tables because some people just sat there with crossed arms. Loggins's mood lifted later, however, as he broke into the classic song "When You Wish upon a Star" just as the roof began opening.

- John Lodge of the Moody Blues threatened to leave the stage because, according to him, too many people in the front row kept leaving their tables and walking in front of him, over and over again.

- Rooney recalls that as he passed nearby the legendary Bob Dylan backstage just prior to the artist's performance, Dylan was overheard to say, "They're eating cheese out there." (I don't believe anyone dared to say back to Dylan, "Don't think twice, it's all right.")

19

THE TROUBADOURS

AN APPROPRIATE WAY TO CLOSE THE CURTAIN
ON THE CIVIC ARENA

BY RICH BOYER

Anticipation. This was the moment I had been waiting for. The third pillar that every Penguin fan knew had to happen to keep them in Pittsburgh was about to be realized. As the lights dimmed and the video started to play, my mind wandered back to my memories of the now vacant "Old Girl."

Catching a fish in the tank at the Sportsman Show, which was held in the basement exhibit space, at my tenth birthday party. Watching my fourth-grade gym teacher, "Sparky Watts," play in a new "adult hockey" league after the Penguin game. Catching a tennis ball hit by Evonne Goolagong after a Pittsburgh Triangle game. Seeing the Pipers win the ABA championship with my dad. The roof opening during the encore of a Crosby, Stills and Nash concert and seeing a column of smoke slowly rise into the night sky. Taking my son to hockey games and watching him stick-handle through the crowds in the concourse with a miniature plastic hockey stick. Feeling the entire arena shake and resonate during Game 5 of the 1989 playoff series against the Flyers. I never heard the arena that loud again after Rob Brown scored two goals in a three-minute span to put the Penguins up, 9–3. Seeing Franco Harris seated across the aisle and forgetting my "Immaculate Reception" program for him to sign. The Red Wing fan who bolted down my aisle with an octopus, throwing it onto the ice and streaking back past me before I could stick out my leg to trip him (probably better that I missed that one). Mario scoring four goals in the first period of the 1990 NHL All-Star

Game and shortly after going on the injured reserve with his first back issues. But the memory that still burns in my mind happened on a warm Saturday night in June 2010.

The Troubadour Reunion Tour was announced on March 9, 2010. James Taylor and Carole King had first performed together at the Troubadour nightclub in Los Angeles in November 1970 and had reunited again at the Troubadour in 2007 in celebration of the club's fiftieth anniversary. The show was such a success that they decided to take it on the road in 2010. I cannot think of two more classy performers to close the Civic Arena, but it almost didn't happen.

"Maxwell and Jill Scott: The Tour" was announced on March 4, 2010, just five days before the Troubadours announced their show. At the time, Maxwell was fresh from winning Grammys for Best R&B Album and Best Male R&B Vocal Performance for his *BLACKsummers'night* album and his single "Pretty Wings." Jill Scott was starting her acting career in an HBO miniseries and introducing her new album, *Light of the Sun*, which was to be released in the summer of 2010. A featured artist, Erykah Badu, and an opening act, Melanie Fiona, rounded out this powerhouse tour. And, of course, the tour opened on May 21 in Cleveland (it figures) at "The Q."

A second leg of the tour was announced shortly after for summer 2010 and included a Civic Arena stop on July 10. The tour was scheduled to end later that summer in Baltimore and could have easily supplanted the Troubadours, with Maxwell's rather dark song "Pretty Wings" as my last memory.

Time will bring the real end to our trial
One day there'll be no remnants, no trace, no residual
No feelings within ya, then you won't remember me.

With the raising of the Stanley Cup banners beginning in 1991, the hockey gods ruled all events at the arena. But, on June 17, with hockey being nothing more than a memory at the facility, other factors prompted a change in the Civic Arena's final event. The Maxwell and Jill Scott tour was abruptly canceled, Columbia Records citing scheduling conflicts at various venues. But there were rumors of ill will among Maxwell, Scott, Fiona and Badu. Apparently, the ladies were running over their allotted time and showing up Maxwell. In any case, a tour that opens in Cleveland is ultimately doomed, and the last show was June 26 at Madison Square Garden.

Meanwhile, the Troubadour Reunion Tour opened on March 27 in Melbourne, Australia, and was the best-selling ticket in the world during

On August 14, 2008, the City of Pittsburgh broke ground on the eventual replacement for the Civic Arena, the Consol Energy Center (currently the PPG Paints Arena). While the new arena is considered one of the best in the NHL and has been a financial boon to both the city and the Penguins, it pales in comparison to the history that took place inside the Igloo. *Courtesy of David Finoli.*

January. The Pittsburgh date was announced, and the stage was set for J.T. and Carole to reserve their space in Pittsburgh history. The tour ended twelve dates and one month later in Hollywood on July 20.

It was a warm, clear evening as we made our way up the grade to the main entrance. I had left my annual guys' golf trip early to be here tonight and would not have missed this moment. By this point, the "Mellon Arena" was looking a little disheveled and unloved, as usual maintenance had to be canceled due to the impending demolition. Banners, signs and decorations were removed, harkening back to the early days of the expansion Penguins. You could pick up scents of dust, mold, locker room and beer. As we made our way to our seats, an elegant Vegas nightclub set unfolded on the arena floor. It was a contrast to the rest of the "Old Lady." The show was "in the round," with an elevated circle stage in the middle surrounded by circular tables for six, each with a candelabra in the center. At that point I got the question from my wife as to why we did not have those pretty floor seats.

Always a quick wit, I responded that they were VIP seats and were sold out. I doubt she bought any of that, but thankfully, we did have a good vantage point behind the visitors' goal.

As the lights went down, the whole scene and mood underwent an amazing transformation. The candelabras were lit, and Carole King appeared in a black evening gown; Taylor followed soon after in a sport jacket. I remember telling my wife that Carole King was the hottest-looking sixty-eight-year-old I had ever seen, and she actually agreed with me. The place must have looked just fine to the performers, as they had played Newark, New Jersey, the night before. The show was a 100-percent sell-out at 14,302. In old-school nightclub fashion, the show included an intermission. The Troubadours tag-teamed through their many hits—some solo and a few as a duet. Taylor, who always connects with his audience, noted near the end of the show, to a chorus of boos from the crowd, "It's kind of bittersweet. We remember playing here in 1971. They say they are going to shut the old girl down." The twenty-eighth and last song of the two-and-a-half-hour show was "You Can Close Your Eyes," performed without the band with both performers at center stage.

> *It won't be long before another day*
> *We're gonna have a good time*
> *And no one's gonna take that time away*
> *You can stay as long as you like.*
> *So, close your eyes, you can close your eyes, it's all right*
> *I don't know no love songs and I can't sing the blues anymore.*
> *But I can sing this song and you can sing this song when I'm gone.*

We will continue to sing the "Old Lady's" song when she's gone, thankful that the Maxwell tour was abruptly canceled and doubly thankful for all of the fine memories. It was a truly classy and bittersweet close for the "largest retractable dome building in the world." A fitting headline appeared in the *Post-Gazette*: "Folk Giants King, Taylor Bid Civic Arena a Classy Farewell." Not much was said as we made our way out for the last time, into the summertime darkness and the crush of the city.

The video was almost over as I snapped back to reality. The crowd cheered as the old Civic Arena ice was melted, then suddenly, a spotlight was shown at center ice. There was Mario, dressed to kill, pouring melted water from the ice at the old Civic Arena onto the shiny, brand-new ice surface. The connection was made, the memories were enshrined and the new arena was appropriately christened!

PART IV

BASKETBALL

20

THE DAY THE NBA DIED IN PITTSBURGH

BY DAVID FINOLI

As the 1950s were entering the middle of the decade, the Duquesne Gardens was the home of two champions. In 1955, the Duquesne Dukes won their lone basketball national championship, while the local hockey team, the Pittsburgh Hornets of the American Hockey League (AHL), captured the franchise's second Calder Cup. Fans of the Steel City looked toward the old facility for their peace of mind when it came to sports, since both the Pirates and the Steelers were mired in losing eras. In February 1956, their worlds came crashing down—literally. It was announced that the Duquesne Gardens was being razed after hockey season ended. They were dumbfounded, especially since it meant the Hornets would have no place to play.

A new place was being constructed. On February 8, 1953, Mayor David Lawrence announced the construction of a new facility that department-store owner Edgar J. Kaufmann was contributing a million dollars toward. It would be the home of the Civic Light Opera and host other events in the lower part of the Hill District in Pittsburgh. The new place would eventually be named the Civic Arena. Crisis averted; the Hornets would play there. There was just one catch. It would be eight more years until the facility was completed. That left the owner of the Hornets without a proper place to play for five years. The owner, John H. Harris, had no choice but to make a decision that the hockey fans of Pittsburgh did not want to hear. While many did what they could to save the facility, they failed. The Hornets would vacate the Duquesne Gardens on April 30, 1956, and the team, after twenty mostly successful seasons, would be suspended until the Igloo was finished. Since that wasn't to be until 1961, the city was forced to live without hockey for five long years.

Harris was the son of John P. Harris, who opened the first theater in the world dedicated to showing nothing but movies. John H. had his own moment in the sun when he founded the Ice Capades in 1940. Eight years earlier, he had leased the Duquesne Gardens, and after three years of hosting hockey teams that failed financially, he bought a team in the AHL in 1936 and named it the Hornets. The franchise was loved by the fans, as it went on a twenty-year run during which it captured the league crown twice.

When the 1960s began, fans longing for professional hockey in Pittsburgh seemed to see a light at the end of the tunnel. On July 27, 1960, the Public Auditorium Authority, which was making the decisions for the Igloo, granted Harris ninety-six dates, thirty-six for both hockey and basketball and the rest for potential other events, such as his Ice Capades. The AHL had reactivated the Hornets the month before, so it was a certainty that they would return when the Civic Arena opened a year later. But there was something interesting in what the owner was given by the authority—thirty-six dates for basketball. What basketball were they talking about?

Apparently, Harris had applied for an NBA franchise and was all but assured from the league that his application would be approved. There would be an NBA team in the Igloo not long after it opened. The NBA's meetings were in October, and it seemed like a formality. As it turned out, it was a formality. On October 7 in Chicago, Pittsburgh and Chicago were awarded the league's eleventh and twelfth franchises. Their rosters would be filled with an expansion draft from the existing teams' rosters and the collegiate draft.

Remarkably, Harris, who also owned the city's last foray into professional basketball, the Ironmen of the Basketball Association of America (BAA), had done it. He brought not only his Hornets to the Igloo but also the NBA. For fans in Pittsburgh, it was an incredible moment. They'd be represented in all four sports, although the Hornets would still be at the minor-league level. That was OK; the city loved them. And with the Pirates winning the most recent World Series and the Steelers about to go into a renaissance of their own in the early 1960s, the two new teams would make Pittsburgh one of the country's epicenters when it came to professional sports. But a funny thing happened on the way to becoming part of the NBA. Harris soon would unbelievably back out of his ownership.

Shown here is the opening tipoff before the final City Game ever played at the Civic Arena on December 2, 2009. Pitt would go on to win the game against their rivals from Duquesne, 67–58, in double overtime for their ninth win in a row in the series. *Courtesy of Duquesne Athletics.*

One of the reasons Harris wanted to own an NBA team was that he thought he had secured the rights to the Celtics' Bill Sharman to coach the team. Boston owner Walter Brown refused to let Sharman, who eventually won an NBA title coaching the Los Angeles Lakers in 1972, sign with Pittsburgh, and an irritated Harris withdrew his application to be part of the league.

After Harris backed out, deciding instead to move forward just with the Hornets at the Igloo, a man by the name of Lenny Litman quickly came to the forefront. Litman had already secured a franchise in the new American Basketball League (ABL) for the city, but since it seemed apparent that the NBA was coming to Pittsburgh, the ABL wanted to move his franchise to Houston. Litman intended to talk to NBA commissioner Maurice Podoloff to see if he could resuscitate an NBA franchise for the city. While Podoloff seemed amiable to awarding the franchise to Litman, the prospective owner exclaimed in an article in the *Pittsburgh Press* on January 19, 1961: "Then I plan to have a meeting with NBA officials to see what they have to offer. However, I must admit that I'm leaning towards the ABL right now." His reasoning was he'd have an inferior team in the NBA, but in the ABL he'd be starting on the same level as everyone else. He felt he could succeed there quicker. Litman eventual did choose the ABL for Pittsburgh and it was a very shortsighted decision, as the ABL lasted not even two full seasons.

In the end, the Civic Arena started off with the Hornets and the ABL's Pittsburgh Rens, which folded in 1963. But because of Harris's shocking decision and Litman's shortsighted one, Pittsburgh never got the NBA franchise that it seemed destined for. And it has never come close to getting one in the more than sixty years since. It was truly the day the NBA died in Pittsburgh.

21

WHEN ADVERSITY MEETS OPPORTUNITY

THE PITTSBURGH RENS

BY GARY KINN

In early 1960, the Public Auditorium Authority in Pittsburgh and its new Civic Arena had some challenges. Although the Pittsburgh Hornets would be revived and return to play in the Arena in the established American Hockey League, the club would utilize only thirty-six dates over the course of the year. Although other entertainment events would surely utilize the Arena, many forms of entertainment do not provide an assured, regular source of lease or fee income. When the potential owner of a new NBA franchise, John Harris, backed out of an application with that league over a personnel dispute, the Civic Arena was suddenly without a tenant to occupy the new building for a large number of dates annually.

Abe Saperstein was in the early stages of forming a professional basketball league, to be known as the American Basketball League (ABL), to compete with the NBA. Saperstein was in the process of forming the eight-team league with new owners, including George Steinbrenner, who would own the league's entry in Cleveland. Teams would be placed in Chicago; Cleveland; Kansas City; and Washington, D.C. In addition, to compete with the burgeoning California market for all professional sports, the ABL would place teams in Los Angeles, San Francisco and as far away as Honolulu, Hawaii. The last anticipated entry to the ABL was to be in Pittsburgh. Saperstein knew the business of pro basketball. He had been a promoter of the famous Harlem Globetrotters since the late 1920s and was well acquainted with the business of the sport. His new league would be innovative and progressive. It would award 3 points for a made shot beyond twenty-five feet, and the free-throw lane would be widened to eighteen feet from twelve to encourage a more free-flowing form of the sport.

Norman Leonard "Lenny" Litman knew Pittsburgh. Born in the steel town of Braddock, Pennsylvania, in 1914, Litman actually started his professional career as a sportswriter, covering high school sports at the amazing age of seventeen for the *Pittsburgh Press* and *Pittsburgh Sun Telegraph*. Litman was competitive enough to also box as an amateur. The hustling Litman graduated from Pitt before moving into various jobs covering the entertainment world. Litman wrote a story about an entertainer known as Hoot Gibson, and the two started a relationship that would take Litman to Hollywood for a time and an eventual career as a press agent and music promoter. After a short stint in the navy during World War II, he returrned to Pittsburgh and later purchased a music hall with his two brothers at 818 Liberty Avenue in downtown Pittsburgh. Litman had the hope of making his newly named Copa the place to be for fans of top-level musical acts from across the country. He and his brothers achieved this, as performers such as Ella Fitzgerald, Cab Calloway, Andy Williams, Duke Ellington, Count Basie and Miles Davis performed at Litman's Copa. The venue held only 287 seats but could handle three shows a night. Due to television and other changing aspects of society by the late 1950s, Litman's wonderful run in the music business with the Copa was coming to an end. On New Year's Eve 1959, the Copa closed its doors. Although Litman continued as the Pittsburgh correspondent for *Billboard* magazine after the Copa's demise, the hustling promoter from a Pittsburgh steel town was in need of something more significant to do by the early part of 1960.

Cornelius "Connie" Hawkins was a man without a way to utilize his significant athletic talent to make a career and life for himself by the early months of 1960. Although he met and knew organized crime gambler Jack Molinas while enrolled as a freshman at the University of Iowa in 1960, he was never found guilty of any gambling activity. But the expanding investigations into point fixing associated with college basketball resulted in Connie getting banned from playing anywhere in the NCAA. The NBA took the same stance, and the league collectively decided to ignore Hawkins and others for roster spots in the league. Hawkins was already being recognized as one of the best players in the country. He could do anything with his six-foot, eight-inch frame and athletic ability, but he was also on indefinite exile.

Saperstein needed ownership of a team in Pittsburgh. Once John Harris backed out of the NBA, Saperstein saw his chance. Litman and his brothers had a chance to decide on either the NBA or ABL, and they chose the ABL. Litman felt his ABL entrance would allow for the team to be more competitive than in the established NBA. The Public Auditorium Authority now had a tenant for up to forty more dates per year. The newly christened Pittsburgh Rens (short for Renissance), owned by the Litmans, signed Connie Hawkins to a contract in the fall of 1961.

The rest of the story is now known to history. The ABL played only a single full season (1961–62), and the league failed midway through its second season. The Rens went a respectable 41-40 in their only full season, and nineteen-year-old Connie Hawkins was the league's MVP, averaging 27.5 points and 13.3 rebounds to lead the circuit. The only negative reaction to Hawkins in the ABL was an inquiry by some coaches in early November 1961 regarding his eligibility, due to an obscure rule that may have stated that he wasn't eligible to play until four years of traditional college had passed. But the challenge was eventually overruled.

Pro basketball significantly trailed baseball, football and boxing in the early 1960s for fan interest. Primarily as a result of this, the Rens and the ABL failed. The league had no TV contract and limited exposure. The Rens lost a reported $94,532 in 1961–62, an amount that translates to over $900,000 today. It was later determined that the Litmans also ran into financial difficulties early in their ownership and the team was actually being funded by two other owners in the league for stretches of the two seasons. It would be five years before basketball fans would get to see the sensational Hawkins in action in Pittsburgh again. The Pittsburgh Rens were the result of four parties merging their individual needs to bring professional basketball to the city and the Civic Arena.

22

THE HAWK MAKES HIS MARK ON THE 'BURGH

THE STORY OF THE PITTSBURGH PIPERS

BY JOSH TAYLOR

In a sports-rich city like Pittsburgh where the success of professional franchises like the Pirates, Steelers and Penguins are well-documented, the Pipers are a team lost among the larger entities. The story is a star-crossed ballad of a group led by Hall of Famer Connie Hawkins and the last pro team to clinch a league championship inside the Civic Arena. But the events following that title run altered the course of basketball history in Pittsburgh.

Cornelius "Connie" Hawkins, a Brooklyn native, became a New York prep legend both on the hardwood in the Public Schools Athletic League and on the black-topped courts at Rucker Park, the legendary court in Harlem known for its elite summer streetball tournament. After being named a *Parade* All-American in his senior season, he accepted a scholarship to play at the University of Iowa.

According to David Wolf's biography, *Foul!*, Hawkins met a New York lawyer named Jack Molinas the summer before his freshman year at Iowa. During his first semester, Hawkins struggled with both his grades and finances, having fallen behind $200 in school fees. He reached out to Molinas, who gave him $250 in cash, which Hawkins promised to repay. Four months later, however, Hawkins was mired in what became known as the 1961 college basketball scandal.

Despite having never played a single NCAA basketball game (freshmen were ineligible in those days), Hawkins was alleged to be part of a point-shaving conspiracy that Molinas and several other financiers were involved in. As a result, Hawkins was expelled from Iowa and banned from the

NBA. With his pro basketball dreams perhaps irreparably dashed, he joined the Pittsburgh Rens of the American Basketball League. He was named the league's Most Valuable Player in 1962, but after the ABL folded less than a year later, Hawkins spent the next four years traveling with the world-famous Harlem Globetrotters. Meanwhile, his basketball fortunes were about to change.

The American Basketball Association played its inaugural season in fall of 1967 with eleven teams. The ABA played a more up-tempo game than its counterpart, including a 3-point line—which the NBA did not adopt for another decade—and a thirty-second shot clock (as opposed to the NBA's twenty-four seconds). In addition to the rule changes, the ABA used a red, white and blue leather ball, far more colorful and easier to follow than the NBA's standard orange ball. In February of that year, entertainment promoter Gabe Rubin led a group to create the Pittsburgh Pipers. Meanwhile, in the midst of a $6 million lawsuit against the NBA, Hawkins had left the Globetrotters and moved to Pittsburgh's North Side with his wife, Nancy. Rubin and the Pipers offered Hawkins a contract, and—thanks to some skilled work by his lawyer to keep the option of joining the NBA alive should he win his lawsuit—Hawkins agreed.

The Pipers, led by head coach Vince Cazzetta, took the court for their inaugural season with Hawkins as their star center. But the team did not have a lot of local support. The Pipers shared the Civic Arena with the fellow upstart Pittsburgh Penguins of the National Hockey League. Unlike the Pipers, the Penguins had a considerably bigger following, thanks to the nearly three-decade tenure of their predecessors, the Pittsburgh Hornets of the American Hockey League. The Pipers started the season with an 11-12 record and barely two thousand fans in the stands for any of their home games, but then they made a trade with the New Jersey Americans (now the Brooklyn Nets) that gave their roster exactly what it needed.

The number-one overall pick in the 1963 NBA Draft by the New York Knicks, forward Art Heyman was out of the league after five seasons, but he became a perfect fit with his new Pipers teammates. Heyman, Hawkins and point guard Charles Williams created a trio that averaged 20-plus points per game apiece. After the trade, the Pipers won fifteen straight games and eighteen out of nineteen while slowly but steadily winning over fans in Pittsburgh. By the end of the season, they had a league-best record of 54-24, while Hawkins was the league's leading scorer and later its Most Valuable Player.

The playoffs came, and the Pipers showed no signs of slowing down, sweeping the Indiana Pacers in three games and beating the Minnesota

Pictured here is the trophy presented by the American Basketball Association to the Pittsburgh Pipers after they captured the league's first championship in 1968 with an exciting victory against the New Orleans Buccaneers in seven games. Unfortunately, after the season, the Pipers moved to Minnesota. *Courtesy of David Finoli.*

Muskies, four games to one, in the Eastern Division Finals. They met the New Orleans Buccaneers in the ABA Finals, led by all-stars Doug Moe and Larry Brown. The fiercely contested series went back and forth, with the two teams splitting the first four games. Hawkins missed Game 5 with a knee injury, and the Bucs won at the Civic Arena, 111–108, forcing an elimination game for the Pipers on the road. Hawkins suited up for Game 6 and, with a heavily taped knee, scored 41 points with 12 rebounds to help the Pipers win, 118–112, and force Game 7 back in Pittsburgh.

On the night of May 4, 1968, nearly twelve thousand fans filed into the Civic Arena for Game 7. With a larger crowd finally on their side, every Piper starter scored in double figures, and Hawkins nearly recorded a triple-double (20 points, 13 rebounds, 9 assists) in a 122–113 victory. Written off as another team doomed to fail in a city starved for a winner, and led by a man unfairly ostracized by the basketball world, the Pittsburgh Pipers were champions. But their pinnacle was soon followed by their downfall.

Perhaps the lack of celebration around the Pipers' championship run was a foreshadowing of the team's future: over the summer, the team moved to Minnesota, replacing the departed Muskies. Halfway through the team's first season in Minnesota, Hawkins's NBA ban was lifted, and he left the Pipers to join the Phoenix Suns. A year later, the team returned to Pittsburgh, but without their original star player they never regained the footing they once had. At the start of the 1970 season, they were rebranded as the Condors, but by the end of the following season, the team was dissolved. In 1976, the ABA merged with the NBA, creating a twenty-two-team league, with none in Pittsburgh.

Could there have been an NBA franchise in Pittsburgh had the Pipers stayed? We will never know, but the legacy of the team that took Pittsburgh to the top of the basketball world remains intact, as does the Hall of Fame career of its centerpiece, Connie Hawkins, who was inducted into the Naismith Memorial Basketball Hall of Fame in 1992. In a city known more for its championship teams donning black and gold, the orange and blue of the Pipers will forever stand alone, both chromatically and in the annals of Pittsburgh sports history.

23

THE SAD, STRANGE TALE
OF THE PITTSBURGH CONDORS

BY FRANK GARLAND

In terms of longevity, the Pittsburgh Condors barely register as a blip on the radar screen of professional basketball history.

A direct descendant of the Pittsburgh Pipers and named after an endangered bird species, the Condors played just two seasons in the Civic Arena before becoming extinct in June 1972.

But they certainly generated their share of attention during their brief existence. A name-the-team contest lawsuit, front office and coaching changes, rumored relocations and cloak-and-dagger efforts to lure big-name players were just a few of the reasons the Condors found themselves splashed on local sports pages.

The Condors weren't even supposed to be the Condors when Pittsburgh's ABA franchise took the Civic Arena court for the 1970–71 season. The team, which returned to Pittsburgh after one season in Minneapolis and played the 1969–70 season as the Pipers, was sold in April 1970 to a subsidiary of Haven Industries, a conglomerate that owned Jack Frost sugar, among other things.

Seeking a fresh start and vowing to dig into their deep pockets, the new owners rolled out a fan contest to name the team. The winner would earn $500 and a pair of lifetime seats. A month later, the nameless team appeared to finally have a new identity: the Pioneers, a name submitted by Donald Seymour, a local law school student.

Seen tipping in a shot while at the University of Toledo, John Brisker would go on to be one of the lone shinning stars of an otherwise horrid Pittsburgh Condor franchise in the early 1970s. He would score 26.1 points per game for the American Basketball Association club between 1969 and 1972. *Courtesy of the University of Toledo Athletics.*

There was just one catch. Well, two. First, what was then Point Park College had been using the nickname "Pioneers," and school officials hinted that a lawsuit might be forthcoming. Second, a Wexford woman named Angela Weaver didn't just hint about filing a lawsuit—she actually filed one in Common Pleas Court, claiming that she, not Seymour, should be declared the contest winner. Weaver maintained that the contest rules limited entrants to twenty-five words and that Seymour's entry exceeded that by more than twenty words. "If they wanted a novel," Weaver told the *Pittsburgh Press*, "they should have said so."

Within a couple of weeks, the Pioneers were no more; new head of basketball operations Marty Blake announced the team would be known as the Condors, North America's largest land bird. A few days later, in early August, the club convened for its first week of practice. Among those who made a big impression was top draft choice Mike Maloy, a six-foot, seven-inch All-American from Davidson who had signed a three-year, $150,000 contract. Officials had hoped Maloy would be a force inside, but he proved to be a force only with a knife and fork, as he reported to camp fifty pounds overweight. He was sold to the Virginia Squires in late October.

It wasn't much longer before Blake himself would be headed out of town, as the club ousted him as team president and general manager in mid-January 1971 and replaced him with Mark Binstein, a former West Point cadet. This all unfolded days after word leaked about a secret draft that the ABA had held, in which the Condors selected Villanova star Howard Porter. At the same time, the Condors were secretly wooing former Piper star Connie Hawkins, who had left town to play for the NBA's Phoenix Suns after leading the Pipers to the ABA's first title in 1968. Binstein denied that the Condors were interested, but the *Pittsburgh Press* reported in mid-March that it was "almost certain" the beloved Hawk would return to his professional nest. Alas, he would not, and Porter never suited up in a Condor uniform, either, despite the club's claim that he had signed a valid contract.

Amid the front-office shuffling, secret drafts and behind-the-scenes wheeling and dealing, the Condors struggled on the court, finishing 36-48 and out of the playoffs while averaging only around 2,800 fans per game. There were a few bright spots, though. Stew Johnson, a six-foot, eight-inch forward from nearby Clairton exploded for an ABA record 62 points in a game against the Floridians. And six-foot, five-inch guard/forward John Brisker, the nastiest player in all of professional basketball, was named to the All-ABA's second team after averaging 29.3 points per game.

John Brisker was a two-time all-star for the Pittsburgh Condors in 1971 and 1972. He would go on to play for the Seattle SuperSonics in the NBA. After his career, it was reported that he went to Uganda as a mercenary. He disappeared in Uganda and was declared legally dead in 1985 after being missing since 1978. *Courtesy of the University of Toledo Athletics.*

The Condors played one more season in the Civic Arena, again missing the playoffs with a 25-59 record. They could not even get through the preseason without controversy, suing the NBA's Milwaukee Bucks for breach of contract after they held megastar Kareem Abdul-Jabbar out of the lineup for an exhibition game. The cash-strapped Condors had guaranteed the Bucks $25,000 for the visit, and the 9,888 fans who showed up to the Arena to see Abdul-Jabbar were none too pleased. Neither were the Condors. "We didn't pay $25,000 for Bob Dandridge," an unnamed team official told the *Pittsburgh Press*.

The hits just kept coming for the Condors; two days later, the bruising Brisker was arrested and charged with aggravated assault and battery, resisting arrest and disorderly conduct after refusing to leave a taxi near Three Rivers Stadium during a World Series game between the Pirates and Baltimore Orioles. Ultimately, he would be fined $100 for disorderly conduct but was cleared of the aggravated assault and battery charge.

Another sale rumor surfaced; this one had the club moving to Washington, D.C., but nothing came of it except yet another breach of contract lawsuit filed by the Condors. And more disruption occurred on the basketball side of things as Binstein replaced coach Jack McMahon in early November. He became the franchise's eighth coach in five years.

As the Condors limped to the finish, more sale rumors flared, with El Paso, San Diego, Albuquerque, Omaha and New Haven mentioned as potential landing spots. The final home game of the season—and franchise history—drew an announced crowd of 1,050, but the *Press* announced the turnout as "681 pallbearers at the House of Grief, the Civic Arena." In a most fitting ending, organist Vince Lascheid played "Taps."

By mid-June, it was official: the ABA officially purchased the Condors and the Floridians from their respective owners, and players were dispersed to the league's remaining teams. Brisker wound up in Seattle, playing for the NBA's SuperSonics, where he spent three seasons and averaged just under 12.0 points per game—a far cry from his ABA average of 26.1 in three seasons in Pittsburgh.

Brisker's fate has been the subject of much speculation over the years. Seattle waived him before the 1975–76 season, and in 1978, he reportedly traveled to Africa to enter the import-export business. That would be the last time his family heard from him. Some claim he came under the spell of Ugandan dictator Idi Amin and later was executed by Amin's enemies. No one ever solved the mystery, but Washington State declared Brisker dead in 1985 at age thirty-eight.

There was no mystery regarding the Condors' demise. At least that's the way Frank Gilbert, the club's director of marketing and promotions, saw it nearly fifty years later: "Short on fans. Short on money. And we weren't very good."

24

THE DAPPER DAN ROUNDBALL CLASSIC

HIGH SCHOOL BASKETBALL TAKES CENTER STAGE

BY FRANK GARLAND

Marino Parascenzo remembers the phone call as if it were yesterday. A sportswriter at the *Pittsburgh Post-Gazette*, Parascenzo had a rare evening off, and he and his wife, Leona, were in their Point Breeze apartment, about to sit down to a splendid dinner.

"Leona had some T-bones sizzling, and I had a good martini going," Parascenzo recalled. "The damn phone rings, and it's this guy. 'You don't know me, but I want to talk to you.'"

The "guy" was a teacher from Trafford named John "Sonny" Vaccaro. Although he hadn't played much basketball himself, he had an idea for a high school all-star game—one that would pit the best players in Pennsylvania against the rest of the nation. It was September 1964, and nothing like it had ever been done before.

"I remember telling Leona, 'This guy's a nut, but he has a hell of an idea.'"

Parascenzo couldn't have been more right. Vaccaro's idea, which he conceived with his boyhood pal from Trafford, Pat DiCesare, came to life the following spring as the Dapper Dan Roundball Classic. For twenty-seven years, the Dapper Dan Club—the charity arm of the *Post-Gazette*—sponsored the event, which also included a preliminary contest that matched the Western Pennsylvania Interscholastic Athletic League against the City-Catholic stars. The Dapper Dan Club pulled its sponsorship after the 1991 game, but the Roundball Classic continued for three more years before its run at the Civic Arena came to an end.

Pitt star Sam Clancy (15), who had an outstanding game in the 1977 Dapper Dan contest, comes through with an intimidating slam dunk. One of the best basketball players in the program's history, Clancy eventually made his mark in professional football for Cleveland and Indianapolis in the NFL and Memphis and Pittsburgh in the USFL. *Courtesy of the University of Pittsburgh Athletics.*

The game attracted the best and brightest schoolboy hoop stars in the country, at least until fast-food giant McDonald's got into the all-star business in the late 1970s and ultimately surpassed the Roundball Classic in terms of its ability to lure big-name players. But for years, the Roundball Classic was a must-see event for anyone with an interest in high school basketball.

The first year, though, no one was quite sure how the public would embrace it—at least until the first stories appeared in the *Post-Gazette* in mid-February 1965. "As soon as that first announcement was made, our ticket orders exploded," DiCesare recalled. "I think we sold 9,000 tickets almost immediately."

And to think that Vaccaro, who ultimately became one of the most influential people in the history of basketball through his work with major shoe companies such as Nike, Adidas and Reebok, originally wanted to play the game at McKeesport High School. And rather than have Pennsylvania take on the United States, Vaccaro was thinking of something on a much smaller scale—an all-star game pitting the best of the WPIAL against the best of the City-Catholic leagues.

But his buddy DiCesare told him they needed to take a chance and aim higher. DiCesare knew all about aiming high—and taking chances; he had borrowed $5,000 from his father to help fellow promoter Tim Tormey bring the Beatles to the Civic Arena in September 1964, and that show launched a successful business career for DiCesare. When he and Vaccaro began brainstorming ideas, DiCesare said he told his pal, "'I want to do the Beatles of basketball.' And Sonny said, 'Well, we could try Pennsylvania playing the U.S.'"

Vaccaro's phone call to Parascenzo quickly led to a meeting with *Post-Gazette* sports editor Al Abrams, who was president of the Dapper Dan group. The pitch was that the game could raise money for the group's charitable causes. Despite not being much of a basketball fan, Abrams went along with the idea. And on the night of that first game, March 26, 1965, Parascenzo and Vaccaro walked around the arena and stared up at the crowd in disbelief. "There were 10,334 people there," Vaccaro recalled. "I said [to Parascenzo], 'Look what we did, Marino. Look what we did.' I'll never forget it. I went from this kid from Trafford—Pat and I both—to people who were on a climb to start a whole new world in basketball. This kind of thing had never been done before."

Vaccaro was in charge of selecting the rosters, and he proved to be a wizard in that regard. More than a half dozen Roundball alumni are enshrined in the Naismith Memorial Basketball Hall of Fame in Springfield, Massachusetts, including Shaquille O'Neal, Patrick Ewing, Moses Malone and Dominique Wilkins. Numerous alums have played in the NBA, including Schenley grad Maurice Lucas, who is on Vaccaro's short list of the Roundball's best competitors.

One luminary who helped secure the game's future is Hall of Famer Calvin Murphy, a five-foot, nine-inch guard from Connecticut who went on

Bruce Atkins was a powerful force underneath the basket for the Duquesne Dukes between 1978 and 1982. His battles with Sam Clancy of the University of Pittsburgh were legendary parts of the history of the city game. Atkins played in the 1978 Roundball Classic and was named the MVP for the Pennsylvania All-Star team. *Courtesy of Duquesne Athletics.*

to become an All-American at Niagara and averaged nearly 18 points per game in a thirteen-year NBA career. Murphy put on a show in 1966, scoring 37 points to enthrall a crowd of 9,587. On the Pennsylvania side that year, the equally diminutive Sam Iacino of Farrell nearly matched Murphy, as he poured in 29 points in the U.S. team's 114–106 victory.

"The first year was a great game and [Pennsylvania] won," Vaccaro said, referring to the Pennsylvania stars' 89–76 inaugural victory. "But the game that was the most important to the Roundball was the Calvin Murphy game. He was the first dynamic great player. He and Sammy Iacino put on a show. That was the night that will live forever in Pittsburgh's mind. There's no question that the Calvin Murphy game sold tickets for twenty-five more years."

Another memorable installment was the 1977 classic, which the Pennsylvania stars won, 98–92, before 16,649 people—the largest gathering ever to watch an indoor sporting event in Pittsburgh. Future Duke star Gene Banks won the Most Valuable Player award, but he handed it over to Brashear star Sam Clancy, who would go on to a standout basketball career at Pitt before playing defensive end for the NFL's Cleveland Browns and Indianapolis Colts. "The Clancy/Banks game will be remembered by everyone who saw it—and the ones who pretend they saw it," Vaccaro said.

For years, the Roundball was a must-see event. Crowds in the 13,000s were the norm into the mid-1970s, and when the Arena expanded its seating capacity, the crowds grew even larger—three straight years in the 16,000s. But the magic run ended in the mid-1990s. Pennsylvania's once-gushing talent pipeline began producing fewer stars, and the state could no longer compete against the rest of the nation one-on-one. But those involved will never forget the games or the impact it had on the community and basketball as a whole for the better part of three decades. And they'll never forget the people involved.

"Sonny got the players," Parascenzo recalled. "Pat did the business side. It was a perfect match for those two—you could tell by the results. I don't know that we ever had a kid who wasn't exactly as billed. The kids were fabulous. The great thing about it was, everything was so genuine. You knew from the effort of the people involved, this was a genuine game."

25

THE EASTERN EIGHT TOURNAMENT

BEFORE IT ALL BUSTED UP

BY JOSH TAYLOR

Before the days when conference expansion and large power conferences changed the landscape of college athletics, regional rivalries still held sway and had cachet with major athletic programs. Particularly among proximate rivals Pitt, Penn State and West Virginia, there was one time every year when regional bragging rights weren't the only thing at stake, and the opportunity for each team to write their own postseason destiny upped the ante: the Eastern Eight men's basketball tournament. For half a decade, Pittsburgh's Civic Arena was the epicenter of one of the most competitive and heated conference championships in the nation.

Originally known as the Eastern Collegiate Basketball League, the eight-team conference was formed in 1975, with conference play beginning in 1976. The original eight charter members were Duquesne, George Washington, Massachusetts, Penn State, Pittsburgh, Rutgers, Villanova and West Virginia. After the league's first season, other sports were added, and the name was changed to the Eastern Athletic Association, but it became known as the Eastern Eight.

The inaugural Eastern Eight men's basketball tournament was held at the Spectrum in Philadelphia in 1977, with John Cinicola's Duquesne Dukes facing Hall of Famer Rollie Massimino and Villanova in the championship game. Duquesne point guard Norm Nixon, the conference Player of the Year that season, led the Dukes with 27 points as they beat the Wildcats, 57–54. Nixon, named the tournament's Most Valuable Player, went on

One of the greatest basketball players in Duquesne University history was B.B. Flenory (15), shown here dribbling in a game against Marquette. Flenory is the only *Parade* All-American to ever to play for the Dukes and was selected to the school's All-Century Team. *Courtesy of Duquesne Athletics.*

to be selected twenty-second overall in the 1977 NBA Draft and won two championships in his career with the Los Angeles Lakers.

With the tournament shifting venues from eastern Pennsylvania to the western side of the state in 1978, the four programs in proximity to the Civic Arena—Pitt, Duquesne, West Virginia and Penn State—were given the advantage of a stronger fan presence than the other four teams traveling from the East Coast. But there was a novelty about the 1978 tournament:

it was the last time all eight teams would play in the same venue for the tournament's entirety. Starting the following season, first-round games were played at campus sites.

Massimino and Villanova atoned for the previous season, spoiling both Penn State and Pitt on the way to the conference final against West Virginia. The Wildcats would secure the first of two Eastern Eight titles in three years, beating the Mountaineers, 63–59, with freshman forward Alex Bradley, one of three Villanova players who would later play in the NBA, earning MVP honors.

With a Rutgers championship win in 1979 sandwiched between Villanova's two Eastern Eight titles, the 1981 tournament championship was the only one to feature the two schools that occupied the same area code as the Civic Arena: Pitt and Duquesne. Having split their two meetings during the regular season, the conference title game also became the grudge match between two programs moving in different directions.

The 1980–81 season was one of only two winning seasons in the decade for Duquesne, which had been conference champions just four years prior. With the Dukes having held the head-to-head advantage in the two previous decades, the 1980s were deadlocked at that point, with both teams having won four games apiece. Bolstered by massive senior forward Sam Clancy, along with tournament MVP Lenny McMillan and Clyde Vaughan, Pitt asserted its dominance in the rivalry, winning the conference title game, 64–60. It was the first of nine consecutive wins for the Panthers over their neighbors on the Bluff, eventually winning thirty-six of the next forty meetings between the two.

As the calendar turned to the following year, relations among the eight clubs began to turn colder. Penn State left in 1979 and then returned three years later, and Villanova left the conference after the 1979–80 season to join the Big East. So Pitt decided to follow Villanova, creating resentment among the remaining programs. *Pittsburgh Post-Gazette* columnist Bob Smizik described how much of an effect the soured relationship had on the season.

Pitt was leaving the Eastern Eight to join the Big East, and the other schools didn't like it. The opposing coaches made their unhappiness known in their voting for the conference all-star teams. The case could have been made that Pitt's Clyde Vaughan was the league's player of the year. He led the league in points and rebounds. Yet, he did not make first team. Guard Dwayne Wallace, who led the league in assists, was not named to the first or second team.

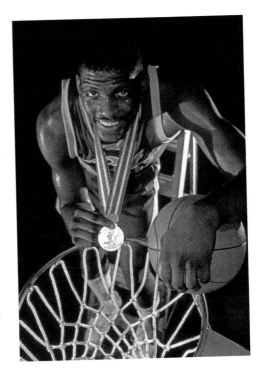

Sam Clancy shows off the gold medal he won in 1979 while playing for the U.S. basketball team at the Pan-Am Games. Clancy starred with the Panthers, becoming the first and still only player in school history to register over 1,000 points and 1,000 rebounds in his career. *Courtesy of the University of Pittsburgh Athletics.*

Also adding to the growing conflict was a war of words between Pitt and West Virginia. WVU had beaten the Panthers at WVU Coliseum in Morgantown on February 24. After the game, WVU coach Gale Catlett talked about how Pitt leaving the Eastern Eight might affect their longtime rivalry. "Maybe we won't play them at all," said Catlett, who also referred to the Panthers as "mediocre." "We don't really need Pitt."

Those were words Pitt would neither forgive, nor forget; and they came back to haunt West Virginia when it mattered most.

After winning yet another grudge match against Duquesne in the first round and beating Rutgers in the second round, Pitt was set to face the Mountaineers—the team that had dispatched both Massachusetts and St. Bonaventure by double digits—in the conference championship game.

It was a chance for West Virginia to send the Panthers off with their tail between their legs with a three-game season sweep, but for Pitt, it was about vindication and validation. They would find both in a 79–72 victory in front of more than sixteen thousand fans at the Civic Arena. The Mountaineers, who had lost only two games the entire season before the conference title game, was forced into 20 turnovers, while Pitt shot nearly 64 percent from the field.

The only thing hotter than the Panthers' shooting during the game was the talk afterward. "This game probably was more important to us than the [win against Duquesne] last year," said Pitt head coach Roy Chipman. "I'm going back and look in my dictionary for the meaning of 'mediocrity.'"

For a conference tournament that would never carry the same regional rivalries and the contempt accompanying them, it was the perfect ending of an era. With the addition of Saint Joseph's and Temple to expand the conference, the original name was gone, too. What was once the Eastern Eight became the Atlantic 10 before the start of the 1982–83 season. It was a changing of the guard in the college basketball landscape, but as Smizik described it, "as good as that scene is today, there's still nothing quite like the Eastern Eight tournament."

26

THE CITY GAME

BY JOHN W. FRANKO

Pitt has largely dominated Duquesne in men's basketball in the past four decades, but there was a time when the series was once one of the most hotly contested rivalries in the country. And the Civic Arena was the site of many classic tilts.

From 1966 to 2009, the schools met there thirty-five times, with the Panthers holding a 21–14 edge in victories. But it was the Dukes who dominated the series in the early years, winning twelve of the first sixteen games held at the Igloo.

They first met there on December 10, 1966, in the consolation game of the Steel Bowl. The Dukes won, 72–65, led by Moe Barr's game-high 19 points. The following year, they captured its championship with a 100–66 win over the Panthers. It marked the school's eighth title in the seventeen years of the tournament.

The Dukes took the title once again the following year with a 57–42 win over the Panthers.

On December 29, 1970, a crowd of more than ten thousand at the Arena saw Pitt get its revenge against Duquesne with a 70–58 upset in the first round of the Steel Bowl. Panther sophomore Buzzy Harrison of Uniontown came off the bench to lead Pitt with 25 points.

"I certainly had to admire the way Pitt played," said legendary UCLA coach John Wooden, whose squad would play the Panthers for the title. "Pitt refused to rattle and stuck to its game plan."

Coach Mike Rice (*far left*), a former outstanding player for Duquesne, and Bruce Atkins (*far right*) combined to lead the Dukes to their last championship to date. They were co-regular-season champions of the Eastern Eight conference in 1979–80 and 1980–81, garnering bids to the NIT in both seasons. Both tournament games were played at the Civic Arena in 1980. *Courtesy of Duquesne Athletics.*

The loss denied the Dukes a chance to play the defending national champions. "That was embarrassing," said the Dukes' Jarrett Durham in 2011. "We wanted to play UCLA. We wanted to prove ourselves to the best."

The following year, it was the Dukes who got revenge when they knocked off the Panthers, 87–67, before 10,361 in the title game. They were led by Lionel Billingy's 35 points. "Even though the outcome was one-sided, it was a great spectacle—all the rivalry and the bad blood but still very little incidence of bad taste," wrote Russ Franke of the *Pittsburgh Press*.

The evening featured a pregame meeting between Pitt chancellor Wesley Posvar and "Mr. Duquesne," Mossie Murphy. "Murphy's a good guy," Posvar said later. "He only roots against us once a year."

The Dukes won another Steel Bowl matchup a year later, but the Panthers came back to win, 82–65, in the first round of the 1973 tournament. "Yeah, I guess this means a little more than beating, say, a…," said Pitt coach Buzz Ridl before he caught himself and stopped.

In 1974, the Dukes won, 100–94, in the first round of the Steel Bowl. Many called it one of the most exciting games in the history of the series.

The schools had now played eight straight games of the City Series at the Civic Arena as part of the Steel Bowl. Duquesne had been content with playing the Panthers just once each year in the tournament, but following the 1974 game, former coach and new athletic director Red Manning said that financial considerations forced the school to take a closer look at playing Pitt more than once.

"We figured the Steel Bowl was enough," he said. "But now we have to take another look at where Duquesne is going in Pittsburgh."

Duquesne beat the Panthers, 75–74, in the first round of the 1975 Steel Bowl. Pitt and Duquesne met for the final time in the Steel Bowl on December 11, 1976, with the Dukes taking a 79–78 thriller.

In 1977, Pitt knocked off Duquesne, 64–56. Both schools became members of the Eastern Eight the following year, leading to some of the most exciting games of the series.

On February 5, 1978, the Dukes won, 88–66, before 9,916, the largest crowd in the City Series since the 1970 Steel Bowl. They met again at the Arena on February 1, 1979, when Pitt won, 89–83, before 10,205. The game featured a dual of big men: Pitt's Sam Clancy and Duquesne's Bruce Atkins. Clancy finished with 23 points and 13 rebounds, Atkins with 25 points and 12 rebounds.

"This is what college basketball is all about," said Duquesne coach Mike Rice. "It hurts to lose, but I'd rather lose before 10,000 people than lose before 1,000."

The following season, Duquesne came away with a 67–66 win before a Civic Arena–record crowd of 15,728 in their second meeting of the year. A month later, the Dukes won another thriller there, a 65–63 victory before 12,385 in the first round of the NIT.

On February 15, 1981, Duquesne won yet another nail-biter, 66–64, before 15, 824. "THE CROWD'S REACTION to Duquesne's thrilling 66–64 victory over Pitt yesterday left one thing clear," wrote Pat Livingston in the *Pittsburgh Press*. "This is a showcase rivalry that should be played at the Civic Arena."

Pitt guard Darrell Gissendanner takes a rebound away from a St. Bonaventure player. Gissendanner averaged 10.3 points per game his senior season in 1981–82. After not being drafted by the NBA following his Pitt career, he attempted to make the Pittsburgh Steelers as a defensive back, signing a free-agent contract with them. *Courtesy of the University of Pittsburgh Athletics.*

Less than a month later, however, the Panthers upset the Dukes, 64–60, in the Eastern Eight finals before a crowd of 13,823.

With Pitt set to enter the Big East, the last Eastern Eight League game between the schools at the Arena was held on February 14, 1982. Pitt emerged with a thrilling 69–68 win. The game was marred by a bench-clearing brawl that erupted after Duquesne's Andy Sisinni and Pitt's Darrell Gissendanner came up swinging after scrambling for a loose ball.

But the momentum of the series had clearly shifted. The win was the second of what would become thirteen in a row for the Panthers at the Arena. They won by scores of 64–59, 77–61 and 107–77 before a dispute between the schools led to a two-year layoff.

When the series resumed in 1990, Pitt won, 84–65, and followed it with wins of 93–69, 102–91, 77–66, 76–72, 84–73 and 75–73.

Duquesne finally broke the streak in 1998 with an 80–69 win. The Panthers won, 65–60, in 1999, and 74–56 later that year. Pitt's second win came the day before the Civic Arena officially became Mellon Arena.

"It's amazing—sad, actually—what has become of the once-fierce rivalry," wrote the *Post-Gazette*'s Ron Cook. "It used to be the biggest game on each team's schedule."

The Dukes prevailed, 71–70 in 2000 on an Aaron Lovelace tip-in with 2.2 seconds left.

With Pitt moving into its new Petersen Events Center, it was decided that the 2001 game would be the final contest of the series at Mellon Arena. The series would return to campus sites. Pitt took home a 78–63 victory. "Give Pitt and Duquesne credit for one thing," wrote Cook. "Beginning next season, they will take the City Game from cavernous Mellon Arena and play on campus."

Pitt and Duquesne returned to Mellon Arena in 2009 in the last basketball game (other than a Harlem Globetrotters exhibition) to be played there. The Panthers overcame a 13-point halftime deficit to win, 67–58, in double overtime. It was the first double-overtime game in series history.

27

DAVE AND CHRIS'S EXCELLENT ADVENTURE

THE 1997 NCAA BASKETBALL TOURNAMENT

BY David Finoli

Every sports fan has their own bucket list of events they need to see. For me, the main one was to get the opportunity to attend March Madness. To be able to look at my bracket that I worked so hard on and check off a game that I was watching live was the dream. Alas, the NCAA Tournament had never come to Pittsburgh, and as the mid-1990s were descending on us, it looked like I would one day have to travel beyond the city limits if I was to check this off my bucket list. (Yes, I know that the movie *Bucket List* hadn't come out yet and that there was no such term in the culture, but we all had a list. We just didn't know what to call it.)

The nearest an NCAA Division I basketball tournament had come to Pittsburgh was in 1971, when it was played at West Virginia University, about ninety minutes outside of the Steel City. Since the law prohibited nine-year-olds from driving and my father wasn't a basketball fan, attending the tourney in Morgantown was not an option. As I was reaching my mid-thirties in the 1990s, it still appeared to be a long shot that the tournament would show its face here. The main culprit was the 10 percent amusement tax the city charged per ticket for sporting events. It was among the highest in the nation and something the NCAA did not want to be a part of.

To my delight, my alma mater, Duquesne University, and its athletic director, Brian Colleary, were dedicated to seeing this event come to the city. The powers that be in Pittsburgh decided to reduce the amusement tax, which was what the NCAA wanted to see. When Duquesne submitted a bid to host the first and second rounds of the 1997 NCAA Tournament, it resulted in success. My dream was about to come true…maybe.

I first had to send in my ticket request to Duquesne, which I did as soon as I could, so it was only a matter of time. As I found out in May 1996, twenty-three thousand other fans also had my dream and sent in requests to the school. The problem was that there were only thirteen thousand tickets available through Duquesne. And unfortunately, it didn't matter that I was one of the first, as the tickets were to be given out in a random draw. I would have to wait until the end of the year to find out just how lucky I was. I finally received my letter from the school. I was almost afraid to open the envelope, afraid my dream would be crushed. When I had the courage to open it, the words I longed for were there: "Congratulations, your two tickets for the 1997 NCAA Tournament will be mailed early in 1997."

It was with pure joy that I called my fellow Duquesne alum and close friend Chris Fletcher to tell him that on March 14 we would have an excellent adventure. It was everything we hoped and so much more.

We got to the Arena early, and I decided to wear my Wisconsin Badger sweatshirt—it was the only one I had with the logo of a team playing that day. The Badgers were taking on Texas in the first tourney game I'd have the pleasure to experience live. The shirt proved to be more an albatross than a help to Wisconsin, as the Longhorns crushed the Badgers, 71–58. I pulled my bracket out of my pocket and put an L next to Wisconsin. Not a great start, but hell, I was living my dream.

We thought the next contest would be a rout, so Fletch and I figured it would be good to make plans on what to do between sessions (we'd have at least three hours to roam the city between the second and third games). Number-two seed South Carolina was facing a school called Coppin State. The only time I had heard of it is when they crushed Duquesne earlier in the season, 91–57. But in the history of the tournament, only two fifteenth seeds had ever beaten a number two. Add that to the fact that no team from the Mid-Eastern Athletic Conference—the league that Coppin State belonged to—had ever won a tournament game. Hell, even columnist Ron Cook dubbed Gamecock coach Eddie Fogler of having "a look of future greatness." A funny thing happened to South Carolina's ascension as one of the great programs in the nation. Coppin State coach Ronald "Fang" Mitchell prepared his team to play at a level few if any thought possible. They upset the Gamecocks, 78–65, in a game that was as dominant as the score indicated. Of course, we didn't have time to make midsession plans,

While his career was phenomenal and his contributions to the program are many, Duquesne's B.B. Flenory (15) was at his best at the West Virginia Classic on December 29–30, 1978, when he scored 41 and 48 points on consecutive evenings. The 48 points is still the second-highest figure in school history, while the 41 is eleventh. *Courtesy of Duquesne Athletics.*

as we were completely focused on this stunning contest. It was perhaps the greatest upset in the tournament's history to that point.

Fletch and I were dumbfounded. Not only were we finally getting to see March Madness, but we also got to experience exactly why they call it that. We were pumped. With no plans in hand we decided to walk downtown to the famed Oyster House to grab a fish sandwich (after all, it was a Friday during Lent, and I didn't want to anger my mother). Afterward, we moved over to Froggy's, a popular bar near the Market Square section of the city, for a drink or two. We then went to a cigar bar upstairs and enjoyed a celebratory stogie. After that, it was time to crash an Old Dominion alumni gathering at the old Radisson Hotel where, luckily, they accepted us as their own.

When it was time to walk back to the Arena, we discovered just what a long day the first round of the tourney could be. The third game was our newly adopted Old Dominion team (we promised we'd root for them in exchange for a beer) against New Mexico. The Lobos won the contest, 59–55, in a game during which we both nodded off in our seats several times. We got our second wind for the final contest, in which Louisville defeated UMass, 65–57.

What a day! There was no way the second round could be more exciting. But to our amazement, it was. New Mexico fell just short as the sixth-seeded Cardinals from Louisville moved on to the Sweet Sixteen with a 64–63 victory. Coppin State fought hard but lost to the tenth seed from Austin, Texas, 82–81. In the game, the Longhorns led by as many as 13 points before almost blowing it late in what would have been the ultimate Cinderella story.

The 17,500 fans at the Igloo couldn't have asked for more. It was all we had imagined and more. Dave and Chris's excellent adventure was certainly one for the ages.

28

A PANTHER HOMECOMING

THE 2002 NCAA BASKETBALL TOURNAMENT

BY JOSH TAYLOR

Earning a bid to the NCAA Tournament is what every team aspires to. But it is both rare and fortuitous for a team to play a tournament game in front of its hometown fans. For the Pittsburgh Panthers, that honor came in 2002, when they drew the third seed in the tournament's South Region and played the first two rounds at Mellon Arena, less than five miles from their home court at Fitzgerald Field House.

Under the leadership of head coach Ben Howland and led by junior point guard Brandin Knight—a third-team Associated Press All-American and the Big East Co-Player of the Year—the Panthers personified the long-standing reputation of Big East basketball: tough, defensively stout and physical. These qualities were confirmed by the team's first-place regular-season finish in the conference standings and an eventual program record for overall wins in a season with twenty-nine.

Amassing a regular-season record of 25-4 (13-3 in conference play), Pitt played a game that was rooted in efficiency, which often overshadowed their lack of high offensive output. While ranking 139th nationally in scoring, Pitt was 31st in field goal percentage, buoyed by a 5th ranking in 2-point shooting (54.8 percent). But their identity came mostly from their defensive prowess, allowing the 12th-fewest points per game in the nation (60.9) and ranking 15th in rebounds.

With the crowd at Mellon Arena largely on their side, Pitt was matched up with fourteenth-seeded Central Connecticut State in the first round.

The winner would advance to the second round to face either sixth-seeded California (making the second of three consecutive tournament appearances) or eleventh-seeded Pennsylvania, the champions of the Ivy League. Despite having a distinct advantage, the Panthers' bracket draw was far from a foregone conclusion on paper.

Having won the Northeast Conference championship, Central Connecticut State featured six-foot, nine-inch, 275-pound center Corsley Edwards, who was named the league's Player of the Year. Edwards's size, coupled with his season averages of 15.4 points and 8.7 rebounds per game, made him a less than ideal matchup for most teams. But when he suffered a leg injury in the first half, Pitt took advantage of the opportunity and scored 7 consecutive points on the way to a 29–25 halftime lead.

Meanwhile, Pitt's own standout entered the game with a leg injury of his own. Brandin Knight was limited in practice throughout the week due to a right quadriceps strain. But unlike Edwards, Knight played nearly every second of the game, leading the Panthers with 17 points and 9 assists. As the second half began, Knight raised his defensive intensity, swiping 3 steals in the opening four minutes. After stripping Damian Battles at midcourt, Knight finished off a three-point play with a transition layup and a free throw to put Pitt ahead, 40–27.

"That was Brandin leading and that's why I call him the Einstein of point guards," said Howland after the game in an article by Steve Henson in the *Los Angeles Times* on March 16, 2002. "Great players make plays, and he made the plays."

Knight added a few more signature moments after a rally by the visiting Blue Devils pulled them to within 3 points to trail, 43–40, midway through the second half. On Pitt's next trip down the floor, Knight found sophomore guard Julius Page—the team's second-leading scorer—in the corner for a 3-pointer that bounced off the rim and into the basket to extend the lead. A few moments later, the two connected again on another Page 3-pointer to make it 51–40. Page shot 4-for-6 from behind the arc and finished the game with 16 points in the 71–54 win.

In an article by Phil Axelrod in the *Pittsburgh Post-Gazette* on March 16, 2002, Knight said, "I had confidence he would make the shot. I know if I can get them the ball, they can make plays. It's just a matter of the defense dictating who was going to be open."

It was the first NCAA tournament victory for Pitt since beating Georgia in the first round in 1991. They advanced to face head coach Ben Braun and California in the second round. It was the second time Braun faced Pitt

Brandin Knight was the rock on which the era of championship Pitt basketball was built in the early twenty-first century. The point guard on Coach Ben Howland's teams that went to two Sweet 16 appearances and the program's first Big East Tournament championship, Knight was a John Wooden All-American and had his number retired by the university. *Courtesy of the University of Pittsburgh Athletics.*

in the NCAA Tournament, having lost to the Panthers in the first round as Eastern Michigan's head coach in 1988. The Golden Bears had plenty of length and athleticism, but they were no match for Pitt's stifling team defense. The Panthers used it to keep California from making a single field goal for more than eleven minutes in the second half, and they put together a 16–0 run to take a 44–32 lead with seven minutes left in regulation.

Once again, it was Knight setting the tone with his defense and court vision: a blocked shot and a transition layup at the other end of the floor tied the game at 32. Then Page found his outside shooting stroke, making one of three 3-pointers, followed by a baseline dunk and a jump shot to extend Pitt's lead.

A.J. Diggs finally broke the drought for Cal with a field goal that cut their deficit to 48–39 with less than six minutes left, but then Pitt pulled away with

7 consecutive points to put the game out of reach. The Panthers had four players score in double figures, led by Page's game-high 17 points on 7-of-10 field goal shooting to win, 63–50. Knight added 11 points with 7 assists in another thirty-nine-minute output.

Notching two NCAA tournament wins in their hometown, Pitt reached that total for only the second time in program history (the first in 1974), putting them in the South Regional Semifinal against Mid-American Conference champion Kent State. Head coach Stan Heath and the Golden Flashes were on a twenty-game winning streak, upsetting seventh-seed Oklahoma State in the first round and second-seed Alabama in the second round to set the stage with the Panthers at Rupp Arena in Lexington, Kentucky.

Kent State continued their incredible run, beating Pitt in overtime, 78–73, led by 22 points and 8 rebounds from forward Antonio Gates, who went on to be a five-time All-Pro tight end in the National Football League. But what seemed like catastrophe became a harbinger of progress. Pitt earned a bid to the NCAA Tournament for the next nine seasons, reaching the regional final in each of the next two. After the 2002–3 season, Ben Howland left Pitt to take the head-coaching job at UCLA, and his top assistant, Jamie Dixon, took over the program with the foundation for the future firmly in place. It eventually led to an era of unprecedented postseason success and the most prolific decade in program history.

PART V

WRESTLING AND BOXING

REMEMBERING *STUDIO WRESTLING* AND "THE LIVING LEGEND" BRUNO SAMMARTINO

BY ROBERT HEALY III

Pittsburgh sports fans had it made in the 1970s. Their major-league teams won a combined six championships in that decade's seasons, and the University of Pittsburgh won a national football title. That the region has claimed seven more major titles since then (through 2020) has only added to many fans' short-sighted impression that Pittsburgh has always been the "City of Champions."

Not true.

Consider the 1960s. Of course, Pittsburgh fans were overjoyed seeing their Pirates homer in the final at-bat of the 1960 World Series. But the Pirates didn't get back to the postseason until ten years later, including five years when they failed to even post a winning record.

The town's other main sporting attractions at that time weren't terribly exciting, either.

Longtime Pittsburgh radio man Bill DiFabio summarized the 1960s local sports scene in a 2018 interview in the Washington *Observer-Reporter*, a newspaper serving the area just south of Pittsburgh.

"The Pirates were good in 1965 and 1966, but they didn't win a pennant from 1961 until 1971," DiFabio said. "The Steelers didn't get good until 1972, Franco Harris' rookie year. Pitt football was not very good back then. The hockey team in Pittsburgh was a minor-league affiliate until 1967. There was a championship basketball team in 1968, the Pittsburgh

Pipers, and it had a great player in Connie Hawkins, but nobody went to see them play."

After success in the '70s stirred Pittsburgh pro-sports crazy, it's hard to believe that, at one point, the region wouldn't turn out to see a sports team be led by a future Hall of Famer and compete for a championship. But that was the case most of the time with Hawkins and the 1967–68 Pipers, the American Basketball Association (ABA) champs who played their home games at Pittsburgh's Civic Arena. True, the ABA wasn't the NBA (National Basketball Association), but it was such a good league that it merged with the NBA not long after the Pipers won the title and immediately left Pittsburgh for another city. The Pipers returned to Pittsburgh after a season away but drew even fewer fans than they did before.

The pro sports entities—if you'd call them that—that did draw big crowds to the Civic Arena nearly every time they performed there in the '60s? Professional wrestling promotions, like those with National Wrestling Alliance (NWA) and World Wide Wrestling Federation (WWWF) bouts, led by strongman and eventual WWWF champion Bruno Sammartino.

"There was a time when Bruno was the king of Pittsburgh sports," DiFabio said. "Bruno was the main story in sports locally."

Indeed, Sammartino's 2–1 loss to Buddy Rogers in a best-of-three-falls match for the NWA's World Heavyweight Championship in April 1962 drew a reported 12,474 fans to the Civic Arena (sometimes known then as the Civic Auditorium).

It certainly helped that Sammartino was one of Pittsburgh's own, having immigrated to the city from Pizzoferrato, Italy, as an undernourished teenager after growing up hiding from Nazis. Settling in Pittsburgh's Oakland area, Sammartino ate better, discovered weightlifting and gained, as a young man, regional fame in the 1950s partly by performing feats of strength on a TV show hosted by Pirates broadcaster Bob Prince. A promoter spotted Sammartino and turned his powerful build to professional wrestling, and when Sammartino performed well against the biggest stars of the day, including wowing a New York City crowd by lifting up the massive Haystacks Calhoun, Bruno was on his way to stardom. As was common in a pastime that is mostly scripted, promoters billed Calhoun as being six hundred pounds, though he probably weighed between four hundred and five hundred pounds.

Events with Sammartino—a New York favorite—as the main attraction sold out Madison Square Garden (MSG) 187 times, according to World

Wrestling Entertainment (WWE, née WWWF), 188 if you count his induction into the WWE Hall of Fame in 2013, which prompted another famous "Bru-no" chant from the MSG crowd.

It was at MSG in May 1963 that a twenty-seven-year-old Sammartino defeated Rogers—when the two were competing under the WWWF brand—to become the WWWF's World Heavyweight Champion. That began a now-unheard-of streak of 2,803 days as champ, lasting until January 1971. In other words, the world of sports-entertainment in the 1960s was Bruno's.

Renowned pro wrestling executive and promoter Paul Heyman, in a tribute video from the WWE, put it simply: "[Sammartino was] the greatest champion and box-office attraction in the history of sports-entertainment."

That included Pittsburgh and its Civic Arena, of course, and while exact attendance figures from many of the wrestling events held there aren't reliable, reports indicate that most crowds at Sammartino cards at the Arena during his run as champion dwarfed those of other events held there. Even prior to Sammartino's title reign, he could bring eyeballs to wrestling, especially in Pittsburgh, as evidenced by the April 1962 NWA title bout, as well as his many appearances on a local TV wrestling show that thousands of Pittsburghers grew up with.

"Sammartino put Pittsburgh on the figurative wrestling map," wrote Mike Mastovich of Johnstown, Pennsylvania's *Tribune-Democrat* in 2018, "during his appearances on the local television program 'Studio Wrestling,' which was operated by the Spectator Sports promotion and broadcast on the then-WIIC Channel 11 station now known as WPXI."

Studio Wrestling began in the late 1950s, prior to the opening of the Civic Arena, but it didn't take long for that promotion to put on events at the new venue and include in its shows Sammartino and other local favorites like wrestlers "Jumpin'" Johnny DeFazio and "The Fighting Cop From Carnegie" Frank Holtz, referee Andy "Kid" DePaul, host "Chilly Billy" Cardille and even diehard fan Anna Bopp Buckalew, better known as "Ringside Rosie." Spectator Sports also had success with wrestling shows at Forbes Field and other facilities in and around Pittsburgh.

Sammartino's star power, made possible by his physique, charisma, family-man charm and appeal to Italian Americans, helped establish Pittsburgh as fertile ground for the WWWF. Bruno got his first WWWF world title shot in February 1963 at the Civic Arena. He again lost to Rogers, 2–1, in a best-of-three-falls match, but after beating Rogers for the championship in May at MSG, Sammartino returned to the Civic Arena in June 1963 as a conquering hero and defended the championship by defeating Hans Mortier, 2–1.

That Sammartino had another long run as WWWF champion from December 1973 to April 1977 (another 1,237 days for a total of 4,040 as champ) only added to his status as "The Living Legend," especially in the Pittsburgh area, which remained his home until his 2018 death from heart problems at the age of eighty-two.

"For an entire generation in Western Pennsylvania," wrote Chris Dugan of the *Observer-Reporter* in 2018, "Bruno was Pittsburgh sports before Mean Joe, Mario, Big Ben or Sid."

HELL IN AN IGLOO

MICK FOLEY SHOCKS, AMAZES PITTSBURGH CROWD

BY ROBERT HEALY III

Foley Is Good: And the Real World Is Faker Than Wrestling is the second autobiography by entertainer Mick Foley. No one can doubt the first part. Foley sure was good at what he did, both in terms of professional wrestling and books. As for the second part? The "fake" part? That's always a tough one when it comes to the world of sports-entertainment.

All but a microscopic fraction of pro wrestling's audience knows that the outcomes of its matches are predetermined, as are the soap opera-esque storylines and most of the actors' moves and strikes. But the risks the performers take? And the athletic ability? Those are certainly real. The same goes for a lot of the injuries. I mean, how do you fake one of your teeth—sorry, Mick, half of one—coming out of your nose? Hadn't heard of that? Then you missed what many journalists call perhaps the most famous match in pro wrestling history. It happened at Pittsburgh's Civic Arena in 1998.

A "Hell in a Cell" (think steel cage but bigger) match that was part of the World Wrestling Federation's (WWF) King of the Ring pay-per-view card on Sunday night, June 28, pitted the Undertaker—played by Mark Calaway—against Foley's Mankind character.

The Pittsburgh Post-Gazette's Scott Mervis, when previewing the event, couldn't help but point out the humor, calling Mankind versus the Undertaker "a long-running duel in more ways than one." It turned out that Mervis's play on words was nearly prophetic.

Two moments in the match are so risky and remarkable that Foley, hardly a household name before the event, rode their momentum to become the WWF's World Heavyweight Champion and pen a *New York Times* number-one best-seller, all in the span of the next eighteen months. That was Foley's first memoir, *Have a Nice Day!: A Tale of Blood and Sweatsocks*, the title being an homage to Mankind's catchphrase and the demented, brown-leather-mask-wearing character's penchant for shoving dirty socks into opponents' mouths.

Hey, you either get this stuff or you don't. But before you judge, know that neither that book nor the aforementioned *Foley Is Good*, which also went to number one, utilized a ghostwriter. Nothing fake there, either.

Foley entered the match with a reputation for doing extreme things in (and/or near) the wrestling ring, like his exploits in Japan with a barbed-wire baseball bat or the time in Germany when he lost most of his ear, to name a few. But most of his outrageous moments predated his time in the WWF, now known as World Wrestling Entertainment (WWE). Foley never before had the stage or exposure that the WWF afforded him, and a pay-per-view showdown between Mankind and industry staple the Undertaker was an opportunity to showcase the nearly thirty-three-year-old Foley's showmanship and pain tolerance.

Mankind came down a ramp to the ring area first, but instead of entering the cubed cell, which contained the ring, he climbed its metal fencing and stood on its fenced top armed with a metal chair, awaiting the Undertaker. 'Taker obliged, climbing the structure and meeting Mankind to start the match.

The fence top quickly revealed that it couldn't handle the performers' weight, which was at least five hundred combined pounds. It bowed, and part of it broke during the match's opening moments. Roughly thirty seconds after that first part gave way, the performers made their way to one of the cell's edges, and in what was reportedly a preordained move, 'Taker threw Mankind off the cell and through a ringside announcing table. The fall was between sixteen and twenty-two feet if accounting for its angle, and Foley, who lay crumpled, suffered a dislocated shoulder.

The Civic Arena crowd had a hard time comprehending what it just saw, and Calaway seemingly had just as hard of a time staying in character. So did WWF executive Vince McMahon, who, in a rare authentic moment, came to the fallen Foley to check on his condition.

After several minutes, Foley left the ring area on a stretcher. Then, about halfway up the ramp, he unbelievably got up, smiled, returned to the cell and climbed it again. The Undertaker again met Mankind on the weakened top. He head-butted and punched Mankind (as far as pro wrestling head-butts and punches go), and in an apparently unscripted occurrence, the top gave way again as 'Taker choke-slammed Mankind, this time taking Mankind with it and sending him crashing all the way to the ring mat. Foley briefly became unconscious and still remembers only parts of the match.

"I later asked the Undertaker what he thought when he looked down at me from atop the cell," Foley wrote in his first book. "His answer was chilling in its simplicity: 'I thought you were dead.'"

Calaway, to his credit, was reportedly wrestling with a broken foot. The audience did not know of that injury, but when Calaway jumped down into the ring through its new opening, he appeared to aggravate it.

Somehow, Foley got back to his feet, and Mankind mounted some offense. After Mankind knocked 'Taker down, a TV camera closed in on a bloody Foley, who appeared to be smiling while the infamous tooth could be seen inside one of his nostrils. Foley revealed later that he wasn't smiling; he was trying to show the audience that he was sticking his tongue through a newly formed hole under his lip.

Mankind controlled the next several minutes as Calaway began to bleed from his forehead. After taking 'Taker down again, Mankind, as if the audience hadn't seen enough, went under the ring to fetch a blue bag and revealed its contents, sprinkling and then dumping thousands of thumbtacks onto the mat. In the world of hardcore/extreme wrestling, where Foley had established a cult following before his venture into the WWF, thumbtacks and other torture devices were more commonplace. But for a mainstream audience like for this pay-per-view event, the devices were pretty much unheard of.

Mankind intended to get his opponent onto the tacks, but 'Taker countered, dropping Mankind's back onto them. Foley made sure to roll around, leaving many pins stuck into his body. One more choke-slam later—onto the tacks again, of course—and Mankind was ready for the Undertaker's finishing move, a Tombstone Piledriver (away from the tacks this time).

1-2-3. Match over.

Event personnel again placed Foley on a stretcher, but with some assistance, he got up and walked out of the ring area despite, at some point during the match, suffering a dislocated jaw and a bruised kidney in addition to the more obvious injuries.

The Civic Arena crowd stood and cheered, and chants of "Fol-ey" broke out. "Pittsburgh has a special place in my heart," Foley, who has performed more than a dozen times in the region, told Trib Total Media in 2019. "It's been my best city."

As for his '98 *King of the Ring* performance? "I have met more people over the years [who say they were there] than could have physically fit into the Civic Arena."

Yeah, that sounds like Pittsburgh.

OTHER PRO WRESTLING PAY-PER-VIEW EVENTS AT CIVIC/MELLON ARENA (ALL WWF/E):

"SummerSlam," August 27, 1995: Shawn Michaels defeats Razor Ramon in a ladder match to retain the Intercontinental Championship.

"Unforgiven," September 23, 2001: Western Pennsylvania native and former Olympic champion Kurt Angle defeats Stone Cold Steve Austin for the Undisputed World Heavyweight Championship.

"No Way Out," February 20, 2005: John Cena defeats Angle to earn number-1-contender status for the Heavyweight Championship.

"Armageddon," December 16, 2007: Edge defeats the Undertaker and Batista to win the World Heavyweight Championship.

"Bragging Rights," October 25, 2009: "SmackDown" defeats "Raw," 2–1, in a battle of WWE brands.

GASEOUS CASSIUS INVADES THE SMOKY CITY

BY DOUGLAS CAVANAUGH

Wait until I get to Pittsburgh. I'm gonna talk and talk and talk until I sell every seat in that new arena of yours.
—Cassius Clay

Go out there and knock out that big talking bum, Clay!
—Billy Conn to Charley Powell

Even with only sixteen fights to his record, Cassius Clay was already a master of self-promotion. Some people went so far as to call him "the greatest fistic attraction since Joe Louis." His poetry and endless banter both amused and infuriated everyone. The former wanted to see the spectacle of his predictions of when his opponent "will fall" being realized. The latter, like Billy Conn, wanted to see this mouthy kid get his yap closed. Either way, the tickets sold, and the turnstiles rotated, much to the delight of Civic Arena promoter Archie Litman, who had to outbid twenty other cities seeking Clay's appearance. It was especially surprising considering the inclement weather of January 1963, a thing that usually caused sales to slow considerably. But not in this case.

Al Abrams of the *Post-Gazette* reported, "With the *possible* exception of the 1960 World Series, no athletic event in recent history has caused as much excitement and a demand for tickets as this one."

In truth, Clay was a dream come true for the few remaining boxing men in Pittsburgh. The sport had been dying in Steeltown ever since television started broadcasting boxing in the 1950s and it was no longer necessary to leave one's couch to enjoy a night at the fights. In fact, until the Clay-Powell fight was announced, there hadn't been a real fistic attraction here since the Sugar Ray Robinson–Wilf Greaves bout two years earlier. So, when Cassius began mouthing off and selling seats, it didn't go unnoticed by a few of the old-timers. Art Rooney's bosom pal Patsy Scanlon, a tough former scrapper from the Point, championed Clay for bringing new life to "a tired old game." And local trainer Danny Ryan called all the talk about the upcoming fight "music to my ears" and said it seemed like old times again, when all everyone in Pittsburgh did was talk boxing.

Listen, my friends, this is no jive, Charley Powell must bow out in five.
—Cassius Clay

In football you have to play against 11 men. In boxing it's only one. And I don't think Cassius Clay is as tough as the Green Bay Packers.
—Charley Powell.

Charley Powell was a big, strong football player who had played defensive end for the Oakland Raiders and San Francisco 49ers. He first became interested in boxing at thirteen, when he observed Pittsburgh's own Charley Burley training at a gym in San Diego, California. He started boxing professionally in 1953 and showed better-than-average power right out of the starting gate, running up a nice string of knockouts. Despite Clay's dismissive attitude toward him, Powell's trainer, Angelo Dundee, had worked Powell's corner when he KO'd big Nino Valdez in 1959 and knew how dangerous Charley could be if taken lightly.

Clay held a big celebration for his twenty-first birthday on January 17, a week before the fight. It seemed like every member of the Pittsburgh media showed up to listen to the gabby Louisville kid as he joked, taunted, bragged and recited his now-famous poetry. It was a wildly entertaining performance, none in the audience more appreciative or laughing louder than actor Sebastian Cabot—"Mr. French" from the TV series *Family Affair*—who would be working alongside Clay on a local radio show later that evening.

Powell and Clay both did public workouts at the Sherwyn Hotel. Powell impressed onlookers during his training, especially when he pounded the heavy bag. But it was nothing compared to the Cassius Clay show. Al

Abrams of the *Post-Gazette* was absolutely dumbfounded at the amount of attention Clay brought in, claiming that in four days over three thousand people visited the Sherwyn to watch Cassius do his thing. According to Abrams, even Heavyweight Champion Ezzard Charles and challenger Jersey Joe Walcott couldn't draw half that number to their workouts when they came to Pittsburgh for their world title fight. "Cassius Clay's magnetism has raised the boxing fever here to the highest degree we've ever seen," Abrams wrote. "People, especially women, who never saw a fight before are asking for tickets."

The day of the weigh-in was just an extension of the live theater Clay had conducted all week. The room was packed, and the crowd roared and squealed with delight over the lively verbal antics of Cassius. Powell, who had mostly ignored Clay's taunts since arriving in Pittsburgh, finally began to fire back a bit. Clay was a bit taken aback and angrily let Charley know that he was revising his prediction—now Powell would fall in *three*!

"We shall see," rhymed Charley right back at him, stealing a bit more of the spotlight from Clay.

According to some sources, Powell's brother, who was present at the weigh-in, had had enough of Clay's mouth and challenged him to a fight right then and there. Luckily, cooler heads prevailed, and the two were separated before anything disastrous happened.

I had Joe Louis in his 15th fight here. At this point, I'd say Clay is just as good as Louis in everything but punching power.
—Ernie Sesto, referee

Wait until you see his left jab. Marvelous! And if you thought I was fast on my feet, this guy's speed will blind you. [Clay] will be the next heavyweight champion. In another year, 16 months at most, he'll be able to handle Sonny Liston.
—Billy Conn

Despite the blizzard outside, a Civic Arena record crowd of 11,238 people showed up to watch the culmination of a show so entertaining that it would have made P.T. Barnum sit down and take notes. Cassius poked, popped and darted about, doing whatever he wanted to his muscular foe before stopping him in the third round as promised. The crowd was disappointed, more with Powell's poor performance than anything. But the city itself was overjoyed, owners of hotels, restaurants and eateries reporting record business despite the subzero weather. Cassius Clay had done Pittsburgh right.

As for Powell, he had simply underestimated Clay (as champion Sonny Liston would do a year later). "When he first hit me," he said after the bout, "I thought to myself, I can take two of those to get in one of my own. But in a little while, I found I was getting dizzier and dizzier every time he hit me, and he hurt. Clay throws punches so easily you don't realize how much they shock you until it's too late."

At ringside were such sports luminaries as Pie Traynor, Len Dawson, Teddy Brenner, Billy Conn and Fritzie Zivic. Conn was effusive in his praise of Clay, but Zivic was a bit more dubious about the kid's future, telling a reporter afterward to give Cassius the following message: "Your poetry's atrocious; you are making Liston ferocious!"

But the *Pittsburgh Courier*, like Billy Conn, nailed it on the head when it wrote, "Clay's growing audience may be starting the greatest mass saga in ring history if, by 1963, King Clay will have made a rubble of the current crop of heavies, from Liston to Eddie Machen."

Clay sure seemed to think so, and he remained as cocky and confident as ever. On his way back to his Louisville home, he was pulled over for speeding on the Pennsylvania Turnpike and fined fifteen dollars the next day. After the hearing, he handed a note to ticketing officer Norton Greening. It read: "To Norton from Cassius Clay, next champion. Liston [Sonny] in eight; Doug Jones in five. Good luck, 1963."

32

"GOLDEN" GLORY

AMATEUR BOXING AT PITTSBURGH'S CIVIC ARENA
CREATED LASTING MEMORIES

BY ROBERT HEALY III

Where they go after they leave the tournament is beside the point. They are this year's heroes, the ones to watch."

That was Al Abrams, sports editor of the *Pittsburgh Post-Gazette*, when previewing the western Pennsylvania finals of the 1962 Golden Gloves boxing tournament, the seventeenth annual version of the Golden Gloves in the Pittsburgh area but the first to be held at the city's recently constructed Civic Auditorium/Arena.

Abrams knew the appeal of amateur athletics. The fighters' fame would be fleeting, their accomplishments highlighted for only a short time and perhaps only appreciated in the Pittsburgh area. But the discovery in a community of who among them is strongest and best is too alluring for many sports fans to miss.

"The Golden Gloves have long been billed as the 'Greatest Fight Show Anywhere' without fear of contradiction," Abrams wrote, "because it is entertainment and action par excellence. Add to this the undeniable fact that it is the biggest bargain buy in sports, and you will have the reason for its continuous popularity."

Yes, Golden Gloves boxing, though its hold on the citizenry has waned a good bit, remains one of the enduring ways to determine who western Pennsylvania's tough guys are and a popular community competition for Pittsburghers to watch.

The Civic Arena housed the Golden Gloves' biggest crowds in western Pennsylvania and gave many locals their fondest memories of boxing. Certainly, trading punches (or seeing friends, loved ones or neighbors do that) for local and state championships while representing your slice of the greater region will stir passions. That this was a major-league arena whose same bright lights welcomed Larry Holmes, Floyd Patterson, Sonny Liston and even Joe Frazier, Sugar Ray Robinson and Muhammad Ali only makes it easier to see how Golden Gloves boxing in Pittsburgh sparks sentimentalities.

Robinson knocked out Wilf Greaves in the eighth round of their professional bout on December 8, 1961, in the first boxing event at the new facility. The Golden Gloves made its debut there on February 21, 1962, with the local finals of the amateur tournament billed as the Post-Gazette Dapper Dan Golden Gloves and waged in front of more than eight thousand fans. Teddy Chernoff, 139-pound junior novice from the Bellefield Athletic Club, earned the outstanding boxer honor that night.

The tournament's local finals played out at the Civic Arena for many years, but amateur boxing left there for good in the 1980s, long before the building closed. The state finals left after 1978 and didn't return to Pittsburgh until 2003, when the David L. Lawrence Convention Center hosted. Apparently, amateur boxing no longer drew enough fans to merit use of a facility like the Civic Arena.

"It was way too much money for the size of it, and we couldn't fill it up," said Rick Steigerwald, a former local champ and now Pennsylvania's state athletic commissioner. "Even the pros had a hard time filling it up."

There were also rumors of arguments over gate receipts.

The 1970s and early '80s nevertheless seemed to mark the zenith for local interest in amateur boxing, including Golden Gloves/Belts and Silver Gloves competitions at the arena, owing perhaps heavily to the 1976 *Rocky* film, which inspired boys and young men all over the country to seek glory through the sport. It may have even inspired Chernoff to return. At thirty-six years old and representing the Greensburg Correctional Institution (as an inmate), Chernoff fought through blood, a thirteen-year hiatus from the sport and a twenty-one-year-old opponent to win the Pittsburgh Press Golden Belts March 1982 165-pound open-class championship at the arena.

"Old time fight manager Fats Wingo thought that the Chernoff on the card must have been Teddy's son," the *Press*' Bill Naab wrote.

Christopher Snowbeck wrote a love letter of sorts to Pittsburgh amateur boxing in a July 1998 *Post-Gazette* article, "The 'Rocky' Road," relying heavily on his interactions with legendary Pittsburgh trainer Chuck Senft and Senft's since-defunct Brookline Boxing Club.

"In the 1970s," Snowbeck wrote, "[Senft, who brought recreational boxing to Brookline in the 1950s] started training teens and adults and fielded a team that challenged the best neighborhood gyms in the city. The seasons culminated with the Golden Gloves finals at the Civic Arena, where up to 11,000 people would pay to watch the fights and newspaper headlines would herald a fighter as the 'pride of Brookline.'

"The fans don't turn out in those numbers anymore. This year's Golden Gloves tournament didn't even earn a mention in the Post-Gazette....

"The public opposition to the violence of boxing—to the knuckle-scraping masculinity it seems to promote and the menacing bravado exhibited by an ear-chomping [Mike] Tyson or an obnoxious [Héctor] Camacho—all stems from a lack of appreciation for the amateurs, Chuck said. The glamorous glitz of Vegas and the pros contrasts with the gym at Brookline....The most startling thing about it: There is no ring."

Indeed, a basketball court at the Brookline Recreation Center served as training and sparring space for the neighborhood's fighters, yet the Center's grounds were nevertheless home to dozens of individual and team champions, dubbed "Charlie's Angels" in reference to Senft.

Though Senft is gone—he died in 2016—as are celebrated local trainers Jimmy Cvetic, Jack Staudenmaier, Charles Daniels, James Gruber, Don DeGenther, Bill Zaleta, Carl Riskus, Lee Moore, P.K. Pecora, Spac Dileo, Ray Schafer, Tommy Shaffer, Henry Smith, Red Foley, Mike Bazzone and many others, there remain a number of dedicated people trying to restore the amateur boxing fervor in western Pennsylvania to the level it was once at. The 1978 state Golden Gloves finals, for instance, brought the Civic Arena crowd of over ten thousand to its feet after Philadelphia-area heavyweight Marvis Frazier (a future *Sports Illustrated* cover boy and Joe Frazier's son) defeated Ed Bednarick of the Swissvale Eagles by decision over a hard-fought three rounds.

While those golden days of the Golden Gloves seem very long ago to some, many of that time's top fighters remain in the game, now shepherding the next crop of great Pittsburgh amateurs aiming for championships, their time in the spotlight in rings around the region and their chance to show that they're the toughest guys (or girls) in town.

ADDENDUM: HIGH SCHOOL CLASSIC BROUGHT AMATEUR WRESTLING GREATNESS TO CIVIC ARENA

Dave Schultz is best known for his Olympic gold medal in southern California and his tragic death in eastern Pennsylvania, but western Pennsylvania's amateur wrestling fans also know the Palo Alto, California, product for an event at Pittsburgh's Civic Arena in 1977.

Despite the 155-pound Schultz (not the former Pittsburgh Penguin of the same name) pinning Pennsylvania state champion Mark Barrett of Moon Area High School, Team Pennsylvania defeated a team of American high school all-stars, 29–26, in that year's Press Old Newsboys Wrestling Classic. That was the third-annual version of the famed Classic, which also saw northern WPIAL all-stars defeat the district's southern all-stars, 25–20, in front of nearly six thousand fans.

Referee Paddy Grimes raises the arm of Chris Riskus of the Riskus Boxing Club (South Side Market House) after Riskus won a close decision over Scott Zerbe of the Indiana County Athletic Club at the Pittsburgh Civic Arena on November 16, 1982. The fight was a 132-pound open-class final of one of the Pittsburgh Press Golden Belts tournaments and featured two of the top amateur boxers in the area at that time. *Courtesy of the Riskus family.*

The Civic Arena hosted the event through 1981, and "it earned the reputation as the 'Rose Bowl of Wrestling,'" co-director Kraig Nellis says. It moved to other Pittsburgh locations starting in 1982, became known as the Dapper Dan Wrestling Classic and then the Pittsburgh Wrestling Classic and remains an annual event.

While the United States versus Pennsylvania has always been the Classic's headline matchup, undercards at the Civic Arena included the WPIAL versus Maryland (1975), Ohio (1976), West Virginia (1978), Oklahoma (1979), New York (1980) and Pennsylvania District XI (1981).

33

EVEN THE BEST LAID PLANS

HOLMES VERSUS SNIPES

BY GARY KINN

J ust over thirty years had passed since Jersey Joe Walcott's crushing left hook knocked out Ezzard Charles in round seven at Forbes Field to win the World Heavyweight Championship in 1951. Walcott's win was the last heavyweight title bout seen live in Pittsburgh. But heavyweight boxing would return to the city in November 1981 in a dramatic way. The Civic Arena would also host its first major heavyweight title fight in its twenty-one-year history at the time, and for this one, Pittsburgh would have a number of major figures in boxing at the time on display in the city. In addition, Pittsburgh fight fans got an early live glimpse of a fighter demonstrating why he would eventually go on to be considered among the all-time heavyweight greats in the sport's long history.

Don King, infamous former promoter of Muhammad Ali and George Foreman, among others, announced that a heavyweight fight between current World Boxing Council (WBC) Champion Larry "The Easton Assassin" Holmes and Renaldo "Mr." Snipes would take place at the Civic Arena on the night of Friday, November 6, 1981, scheduled for fifteen rounds. The bout would be televised on ABC nationally, with famed ring announcer Howard Cosell calling the action. Management of the Civic Arena Corporation, recently operating with a new lease to DeBartolo Corporation for the building, reportedly posted over $675,000 to King for the promotion and guaranteed the sale of thirteen thousand seats.

Larry Holmes was not a fighter who chose to take a safe route to retain his title. After starting his career in Easton, Pennsylvania, Holmes had built a 26-0 record with nineteen knockouts before signing to meet feared and established heavyweight Ernie Shavers in Las Vegas in March 1978. Holmes used a solid left jab and his long reach, both of which would become his trademarks, to whip the power-punching Shavers over twelve rounds in a one-sided decision win. The bout set up a date with Ken Norton for the chance to win the WBC title. Norton had won two of his three bouts with Muhammad Ali in the 1970s in the opinion of many experienced observers, though Ali was awarded the decisions, and the Californian Norton was simply one of the best athletes to enter the heavyweight ring. On June 9, 1978, Holmes and Norton waged one of the best and most exciting heavyweight title fights in history on ABC's *Wide World of Sports*, with Holmes prevailing in a glorious back-and-forth, fifteen-round rumble. Two judges had the bout dead even on scorecards after fourteen rounds, and Holmes won the fifteenth round in a gutty performance to lift the title. Holmes then defended his WBC belt ten times prior to the planned bout in Pittsburgh with Snipes, including wins over Shavers again, Muhammad Ali at the end of his career and Leon Spinks, who had earlier conquered Ali.

King had a planned bout already scheduled in mind for Holmes with Gerry Cooney of Long Island, New York. Cooney possessed an usually large six-foot, six-inch frame, a fairly low-key personality and a lethal left hook. The "Gentleman" had piled up a record of 25-0 with eighteen knockouts, including brutal first-round stoppages of Norton and the dangerous Ron Lyle, both also seen on national TV. King saw the lucrative opportunity to match Cooney and Holmes for the WBC title in 1982. He had already started promoting the Holmes-Cooney matchup at the time that the Holmes-Snipes bout was announced. Proceeds for the future bout was estimated to potentially yield over $30 million.

Due to the active dialogue about the potential of Holmes versus Cooney, many in the boxing press panned the upcoming fight between Holmes and Snipes. Despite the financial risks of any upset, and also to stay active, Holmes signed the fight contract. There was no Las Vegas betting line established for the Holmes-Snipes bout. Snipes's 22-0 record was universally questioned, with a controversial decision win over South African Gerrie Coetzee and a split-decision win over Eddie Mustafa Muhammad the only fights with recognizable names on his résumé. Cosell crowed that the challenger "had virtually no chance" of winning as the broadcast began.

When the bell sounded for the bout, Holmes appeared to believe the popular opinion that this was an event just to showcase his skills for the upcoming Cooney blockbuster fight. Holmes came out fast, dominated with his patented left jab and landed numerous combinations to clearly take the points lead during rounds one through three. But at the end of round three, Snipes clearly landed a hard right on a break, which incensed Holmes. Larry came out attempting to finish the fight due to the illegal shot in round four, abandoning his jab and fighting inside with Snipes at ring center. The change in strategy clearly allowed Snipes back into the bout, and it resulted in an action-packed, exchange-filled wild round four. The Civic Arena's 14,103 fans in attendance began to sense some undeniable tension.

Holmes's abandoning of the jab allowed Snipes to build confidence, and the fighters often stood toe-to-toe and exchanged blows again in rounds five and six. Clearly, an unexpected but exciting fight was on. Holmes did open a cut over Snipes's left eye at the end of the sixth round, and Cosell yelled into his microphone that Snipes was showing tremendous courage. But no one could prepare for, nor expect, what came next.

Snipes had begun sneering at Holmes as early as his rally in the fourth. In the first half minute of round seven, with Snipes seemingly summoning the ghosts of Walcott's seventh-round KO of Charles thirty years earlier in Pittsburgh, the challenger landed a straight right hand that floored Holmes at ring center. Holmes's jaw was clipped so solidly that his left knee bent awkwardly as he fell backward onto the canvas. As Holmes got up wobbily at the count of seven, he turned around and then fell forward into a neutral ring corner post, and the padded post is all that held him up. Snipes then forward-pressed for the stoppage, which never came. Larry survived on his feet over the next minute or so, and by the end of round seven, he had fired eleven straight punches back at Snipes in taking back control of the fight. Holmes returned to his jab and took control for rounds eight through ten before stopping Snipes by TKO in the eleventh after landing four consecutive hard right hands near the ropes. Snipes and his handlers loudly protested the stoppage, but Referee Rudy Ortega's call was likely the right one, given the damage that Holmes was inflicting late in the bout.

Many in the crowd also profanely objected to the stoppage, and a postfight melee between camps of the two fighters besmirched the unexpectedly competitive fight. But boxing fans in Pittsburgh got to witness firsthand the excitement of the heavyweight division. In addition, the continued advancement of Larry Holmes on the way to his Hall of Fame career was clearly on display that Friday night in 1981 as he battled back from a hard knockdown to rally and win. In addition, Don King and other current fight promoters still likely recall that straight right hand landed by Renaldo Snipes as current heavyweight championship fights are being contracted and negotiated.

34

A CLOSED-CIRCUIT LOVE AFFAIR

BY DAVID FINOLI

I've never been one who longed for the old days when it comes to technology. I'll take cable TV and the ability to watch the Pirates every night over the alternative any day. Give me a computer and the internet over a typewriter and going to the library to view microfilm to write these books. I can't imagine I'd have the patience with the latter. But when it comes to closed-circuit broadcasts at stadiums and arenas versus pay-per-view in the comfort of my own home, I am the epitome of an old fogy.

Those who know me know how important my Uncle Ed Dilello was to me. He brought me to my first baseball game in 1969—the new San Diego Padres versus the New York Mets at Shea Stadium. (He was irritated with me when he asked what helmet I wanted and I chose a Padre one over the Mets.)

In 1974, he gave me my first closed-circuit experience as the World Cup final was about to be played. He and my aunt Jeannie were visiting from Flushing, New York, and he was a rabid soccer fan who had me look up what facility the final would be shown at locally. I found out it was at the old Syria Mosque, so he took me to see West Germany defeat the Netherlands. I not only became a soccer fan that day but also got a thrill out of seeing a game on TV along with thousands of other cheering fans. It was the closest thing to being there. When they visited again on June 20, 1980, there was another major sporting event going on that he didn't want to miss. Sugar Ray Leonard was taking on Roberto Duran for the World Boxing Council (WBC) Welterweight crown. Uncle Ed took us to the Civic Arena to see the closed-circuit telecast, and a love affair was born. Boxing was made for closed-circuit viewing, and this would prove to be one of the most exciting evenings I had the pleasure to spend at the Igloo.

The arena had a capacity of 16,033 people by 1980, but only 12,500 seats were put on sale for this memorable championship bout. By Thursday, two days before the fight, it was sold out. The demand was such that the experts deemed they could have sold 5,000 more tickets with little effort. It was an incredible back-and-forth battle, with Leonard coming up just short as he dropped a unanimous decision. Half of the crowd at the Arena roared with glee at the decision; the other half booed loudly. It was an incredible atmosphere.

By this point, I was coming off my freshman year at Duquesne, and boxing had become one of my favorite sports. I had never been to a live match, so being in this electric atmosphere drove me to follow the sport more intently. If I couldn't see a live fight, then going to the Civic Arena to see the top battles on the big screen was what I was going to do.

I couldn't make it to Leonard-Duran II, the "No Mas" fight in which Duran quit in his corner, claiming he had a bellyache. (What he apparently had was a pride ache, as Leonard was dominating him to that point.) Next up was another Sugar Ray classic, the first battle against undefeated World Boxing Association champion Thomas Hearns.

The bout was one month into my junior year, and I was having trouble convincing any of my poor college friends to go with me, but this one I wasn't going to miss. I went to the Igloo myself and was happy I made that decision. Once again, the Arena was full in anticipation of a savage battle between these two titans of the welterweight division, and once again, the place seemed to be split as to who they wanted to win. Hearns had been a savage slugger in his career to this point but had put on a technical masterpiece and was comfortably leading Leonard as the thirteenth round was coming to an end.

Leonard needed a knockout to win and hurled between twenty-four and twenty-six unanswered punches at the WBA champion. It was at that point that the boxing world found out Tommy had a suspect chin, as he fell at the 1:45 mark of the fourteenth round in a spectacular fight. The place was as loud as I've ever heard it. This watching boxing on TV with twelve thousand of your best buddies was becoming my favorite thing to do at the Civic Arena.

Two months later, I was finally able to see my first championship bout live, as heavyweight champion Larry Holmes came off the deck to defeat

This is a shot of the court and stands before the final city game hosted at the Arena. The original capacity of the building was 12,508 fans, but with the addition of four upper-level seats in the end zones as well as other construction additions, it eventually rose to a hockey standing-room-only capacity of 17,132. *Courtesy of Duquesne Athletics.*

Renaldo Snipes at the Igloo (a fight told magnificently by Gary Kinn in the previous chapter). But it was Holmes's next bout seven months later against Gerry Cooney that would be my closed-circuit swan song in this famed facility.

I had stayed at Duquesne in the summer between my junior and senior years. When June came around and the fight between Holmes and undefeated Gerry Cooney—a slugger who was being pushed by his camp and the media as the next "white" hope—was to be played on the big TVs at the Arena, I had to be there. It was a scene that was as bizarre as it was exciting. The parking lots were jammed with tailgaters before the fight. The vast majority were Cooney fans, wearing green Irish shirts to show their support.

Cooney was thought to be an inferior challenger, as his 25-0 record seemed to be the result of Cooney being matched up against substandard talent. Larry was, and remains, one of my favorite fighters. I bought and donned my "L.H." hat as I entered the building. I felt I was on an island supporting him.

Early on in one of the preliminary fights, the audio went out as the record Civic Arena closed-circuit crowd of 13,146 turned raucous. Luckily, it resumed within minutes before any damage was done. The bout turned out to be fantastic. Cooney fought magnificently, pushing Holmes hard until the champion finally disposed of him in the thirteenth. The pro-Cooney crowd was irritated with the stoppage and ripped down one of the two big screens that were situated at each end of the floor. Order was restored, and I left the Arena with my hat under my shirt so it wouldn't be taken and destroyed by a Cooney fan.

Eventually, closed-circuit telecasts gave way to HBO, then pay-per-view; closed circuit existed no more. While I certainly enjoyed watching the pay-per-view fights with friends, it wasn't the same feeling I had at the Civic Arena, where watching sports on TV had a new meaning. It's an experience this old fogy misses.

PART VI

OTHER TEAMS AND EVENTS

A WAR ON THE FLOOR

THE CIVIC ARENA WELCOMES...ARENA FOOTBALL!

BY TOM ROONEY

Well into his late seventies, Edward J. DeBartolo Sr. ("Mister D," we called him) was still the first person reporting to the Boardman, Ohio headquarters bearing his name just outside Youngstown. After taking my son Josh to school at what is now called Bishop Canevin, I was one of the first people to arrive at work at the Pittsburgh Civic Arena each morning, timed to getting through Crafton from Washington County and into the city ahead of traffic. Better to be in my office drinking my home-brewed coffee in a thermal cup than riding my brakes headed down Greentree Hill on the Parkway West.

On my phone setting were several button extensions, a couple for me, the operator and "1916," which was the direct line to my boss, Paul Martha. If it rang at 7:30 a.m., it wasn't Paul calling. He was more of a late arrival. It was "Mister D" looking for him, and I better pick up the call. The boss in Youngstown did not like waiting. And Paul's number was on my console to prevent exactly that from happening.

"Mister D, Paul's not in yet, should I give him a message?" I asked a little haltingly, because normally the call was Mister D ranting about another loss for the Penguins. "You guys are behind budgets on events. What are you doing down there, crossword puzzles? Get me more events." The next sound was a sharp click.

Arena football seemed like a good candidate for an event; maybe we could even have a team and get a bunch of home dates. In addition to about forty concerts a year, family shows like *Disney on Ice* and wrestling (Mr. D's favorite: "Man, those people like to eat and drink"), we already had a run of hockey, truck pulls, Duquesne basketball games and selected Pitt Big East basketball games. But booking the budgeted two hundred nights was tough, because the Pens then were not always playoff-bound. So why not arena football? That question was both asked and answered first by the same man.

His name was Jim Foster, and I was glad to take his call. He had dusted off an idea he had in 1981, when he attended a Major Indoor Soccer League All-Star Game. If soccer could be played on a hockey layout, why not football, he asked himself. Before halftime of the soccer game, he had already sketched a layout, complete with the nets around each goalpost where a missed kick could rebound and the ball would still be in play. A replica of the original diagram he sketched on a manila folder he had brought to the game that night resides in an exhibit at the Pro Football Hall of Fame in Canton, Ohio.

Foster was distracted by actually having to earn a living, but he finally got around to testing the idea of arena football in 1985 and then again 1986 in Rockford, Illinois, about ninety miles from Chicago. He had rounded up some former minor-league football teammates to run through some scrimmage concepts in Rockford, playing around with whether there should be seven or eight players on a team. "We paid my buddies with take-out dinner from Burger King and bunked them eight to a room, and the only other thing we promised them was that if there ever was a true league, they'd get first shot at the team tryouts," Foster recalled. It was in Rockford that the local arena manager had gone straight to an industrial supplier, ROHN Towers, to order parts to use to construct goalposts with the nets attached to them that became associated with the creation of arena football. "I walked onto the field in Rockford where they had used the indoor soccer carpet and the netting system, and I was amazed....His guys had translated my vision into reality," Foster recalled. "Quite a thrill!"

In April 1987, Foster was ready to unveil his idea to the world—well, at least to the world of event-needy arena managers like me. My arena colleagues and I had been invited to Rosemont Arena in Chicago. There we were, representing Pittsburgh; Cleveland; Washington, D.C.; Philadelphia; and Denver—guys like me with owners wanting more dates to fill. We were often friends and competitors, this time the latter, like hungry wolves circling to get first shot at fresh roadkill. Foster was ready to roll out what would be branded as "War on the Floor."

"We had a great turnout for that 'spec' game, and it helped that more than four arenas were there, because I had some leverage," Foster remembered when we talked more than three decades later.

Foster had worked in the NFL and the USFL. He had seen owners with big money and big egos spend recklessly to win at any cost, which threatened the competitive structure of the league. So, to avoid the inevitable franchise owner headaches, his Arena Football League would own all the teams as a single entity. He would pick the coaches and sign the players and assign them to teams for balance purposes.

The next step was the deal. We proposed a straight revenue share (80 percent to him, 20 percent to us), with advertising "off the top"—that is, deducted from the ticket sales. Costs on the Arena side were low, because we used the leftover Pittsburgh Spirit indoor soccer carpet after we disbanded them the year before (part of the reason we were so desperate for dates). With concessions, parking and most of local sponsorships kept by us, we had a good chance to make money. That we did.

"I wanted cities and arenas where the operator had strong marketing capability," Foster remembered. "That's why Pittsburgh was included as one of the first four teams. You guys were marketing Penguins, concerts, family shows and other things, so we knew you had the tools. We were happy to go there and have our very first actual game in Pittsburgh."

It was June 19, and advance ticket sales seemed strong. But there was no template for how many people would buy tickets late, an indicator that helped us plan for whether arena football would behave like a concert, in which almost all the tickets are sold by forty-eight hours of the first on-sale date, or a truck pull, in which we could double the advance sale in those last two days.

It was a truck pull. People lined around the ramp from the main entrance box office. A crowd of 12,177 attended to see the hometown Gladiators eke out a 48–46 win over Washington. Two weeks later, with the team sporting a 2-0 record, 11,807 witnessed a home win against Chicago. And with a record of 4-0 going into the final home game, a throng of 14,644 saw the "Glads" suffer their first loss, 32–31, to Denver.

The Denver loss can be attributed at least to some degree to a decision made to open the famed Civic Arena roof when the national anthem was playing. I heard about that minutes after the game ended from Coach Joe Hearing. He roared at me, "Nice job! At least you could have told me in advance."

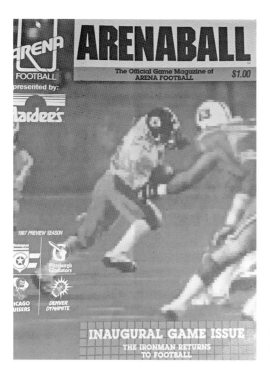

Pictured here is a program of the first regular-season Arena Football League game. It occurred at the Civic Arena on June 19, 1987, as the Pittsburgh Gladiators defeated the Washington Commandos, 48–46, in front of 12,117 at the Igloo. Pittsburgh led the league in attendance that first season, averaging 12,856 fans per game. *Courtesy of David Finoli.*

Denver would return on August 1 to the Civic Arena against an injury-decimated Gladiators and win a blowout, 45–16, and claim the championship in Arena Bowl I with 13,232 attending. "Pittsburgh came up so big for us that first year," Foster recalled. "As a league we actually finished in the black."

Arena Football helped fill the void of spotty Penguin playoff possibilities and the rollup of the Spirit—at least we used their soccer carpet, as did the Pittsburgh Steelers when they were knocked off of their snow-covered and frozen turf at Three Rivers Stadium for practices at the convention center. I have a nice thank-you note from my cousin Dan Rooney somewhere.

"Mister D" was happy enough. And I didn't have to field as many 7:30 a.m. calls on extension 1916, those calls aimed at Paul Martha. But he never really let up on "more dates!" Indoor lacrosse, why not? Roller Derby, yeah, we even gave that another shot.

"Those first guys playing for Whopper sandwiches in Rockford have a little slice of history," Foster said. "They have something to tell their grandkids."

36

IN THE SPIRIT

MY OH-SO-BRIEF AFFAIR WITH INDOOR SOCCER

BY CHRIS FLETCHER

What the hell am I doing here?," I thought, glancing up at the crowd from the "pitch" at the Civic Arena. It's November 2, 1984, and four days ago, half asleep at my job as the news producer for WDVE's wildly popular *Jimmy and Steve* morning drive show, I somehow agreed to be pregame entertainment for the city's Major Indoor Soccer League team, the Spirit. Our intrepid band of WDVE employees and assorted friends of Steve were playing an abbreviated friendly against another team of misfits. I actually wore a headband, which could be forgiven, given it's 1984.

I agreed to this humiliation despite, first, only ever playing soccer in high school gym class with the expressed goal of not getting caught standing around, which would earn you laps; second, not understanding a game in which you couldn't use your hands; third, fearing getting a serious raspberry from sliding on the turf; and fourth, calculating the odds that someone I knew would be in attendance. Also, there would be free beer. *Free beer*—the two greatest words in the English language.

There were about five thousand people on hand for the game against the Baltimore Blast. The venue wasn't packed, but you could hear a little buzz and an occasional conversation. And, of course, one of them was from a beered-up member of the Sheiks, rivals of my Duquesne University group, the Playboys. I hadn't seen him since graduating earlier in the spring. "Nice legs, Fletcher!" he heckled, followed by a chant reminiscent of crowds heckling Darryl Strawberry: "Fletttccchhherrr, Fletttccchherr." So much for being incognito.

But the time I had been dreading turned out to be fun. My soccer career was brief. I was a midfielder, I think, since I could do less damage there. I pretty much ran around without a sense of mission. I managed to bank a pass off the boards that led to one of our two goals. I also whiffed on a kick but redeemed myself with a sliding tackle—and a nasty raspberry. When it was over, we lost, and I was headed for the promised beer.

But a funny thing happened. I stayed for the game and actually liked it. Our group leader in this book project, Dave Finoli, was a soccer guy. I never was, despite his many urgings. Yet somehow this combination of pinball and Dave's beautiful game captured my interest. I decided to give this team a chance. I even used my position at the radio station to parlay some occasional press passes to see a team I had largely ignored.

The Spirit was one of the original franchises in the league, playing in the Civic Arena from 1978 to 1980 and from 1981 to 1986. They were owned first by local beer magnate Frank B. Fuhrer Jr. and then by a mall developer from Youngstown, Ohio, Edward J. DeBartolo. He also owned the Pittsburgh Penguins and the San Francisco 49ers. Crowds were sparse, but in pre-Mario 1983–84, the Spirit actually had a higher average attendance than the Pens.

The Spirit franchise worked hard, because they had to. They were good to the press and generous with free passes. Notwithstanding having the WDVE squad as entertainment, they were innovative in their marketing. This is the group that developed the memorable slogan "We've got 6 guys in shorts who can go all night." They were also blessed with having two stars who were quasi–sex symbols in Paul Child and the best player in franchise history, Stan Terlicki, which might explain the daring marketing pitch.

Most Pittsburghers were like me, late to the party. I missed Terlicki at his finest. In his first year with the Spirit, 1981–82, he was Mario-like. In forty-three games, he amassed 74 goals and 43 assists, earning him MISL co-MVP honors. Finoli would tell me how amazing Terlicki was, how he had a rifle shot from either leg and how he would often take on multiple defenders and make them look bad.

On paper and on the hockey/basketball/soccer court, MISL was perfect for the ugly American sports fan like me. It felt like hockey, six on six, and was faster paced than its traditional outdoor counterpart. And there was scoring. Lots of scoring. The word *nil* seldom if ever applied, unless it was

"What are the chances of my team being shut out? Nil." It was like an Intellivision game (remember, we're still in the mid-1980s here) in real life.

And as for competition, it wasn't the best time for Pittsburgh pro sports. The Pirates were awful and immersed in the infamous "Pittsburgh Drug Trials." The Steelers were on the decline, despite a miracle appearance in the AFC Championship. The last-place Penguins were just starting to generate a true fan base after completely tanking the season before to earn the right to draft a young phenom (that's another chapter).

But it took until 1984 for me to heed the call of the Spirit. I was one year removed from the franchise's best season. In 1983–84, they posted a 32-16 record despite losing Terlecki to the Golden Bay Earthquakes. One of the great names in Pittsburgh sports history, Zeee Kapka, led the team in scoring, tallying 66 points. ("Who scored that beautiful goal? It vas Zeee Kap-ka!") Kevin Maher earned MISL Rookie of the Year honors. And the team lost a hard-fought playoff series to the Cleveland Force, bowing out in four games.

So, when Terlicki returned to the team for the 1984–85 season, there was hope for even the most casual of fans. But it was not to be. The team stunk. I didn't know enough about soccer to know why exactly. Terlicki still led the team in scoring with 39 goals, but the Spirit finished in sixth place, ten games under .500 with a 19-29 record. Despite the awful season, Terlicki did me a solid, recording a tribute for the morning show. "I get a kick out of Jimmy and Steve every morning," he said into my portable recorder. I thanked him afterward. His response: "Whatever, kid."

A few weeks later, I took a job in Youngstown and moved away from Pittsburgh temporarily and from the Spirit permanently. Ironically, my apartment would be three blocks away from the DeBartolo offices in the town's Boardman neighborhood. I was told there was always armed security in the parking lot, but that could have been urban legend.

Back in Pittsburgh, 1985–86 would be the final season for the Spirit. In a year marked by parity and apathy, they finished in last place at 23-25. Yet they would be just four games out of first. Maybe one or two bad bounces off the boards kept them from the playoffs.

After the completion of the season, the franchise folded. There was an attempt to revitalize the team with a new ownership group known as Pittsburgh Soccer Inc., but it never materialized. The MISL itself limped along until 1992 before calling it a day.

For a brief season, I considered myself a fan. But my love of soccer was short-lived. Where have you gone, Stan Terlicki?

37

THE TRIANGLES

PITTSBURGH'S LAST TITLE WON UNDER THE IGLOO ROOF

BY DAVID FINOLI

Much has been made over the years about the fact that Pittsburgh hadn't won a professional championship within the confines of the Steel City since a man by the name of Bill Mazeroski hit a ball over the head of Yankee Hall of Famer Yogi Berra that cleared the left-field wall at Forbes Field to win the 1960 World Series. Since then, the Bucs won two more world championships, both with clinching games in Baltimore, while the Penguins captured five Stanley Cups, all on the road.

When people make this claim, the only teams that are under consideration are the three major professional sports franchises that call Pittsburgh home: the Bucs, the Pens and the Steelers (the latter can never win a league title in Pittsburgh, unless the city somehow secures a bid to host a Super Bowl). In reality, there have been three other professional teams, although none on a major sports league level, that have won championships in the city since Maz's historic long ball. And all have been in the Civic Arena.

The Hornets captured their final American Hockey League title in the last game in franchise history on April 30, 1967, with a 4–3 overtime win over Rochester. The Pittsburgh Pipers rolled over the New Orleans Buccaneers, 122–113, to win the first American Basketball Association championship on May 4, 1968, and the final one occurred on August 25, 1975, in front of 6,882 fans on a warm summer evening when the Pittsburgh Triangles hoisted the Bancroft Trophy by defeating the Golden Gaters, 21–14, to take their one and only World Team Tennis title.

Tennis wasn't made to be a season-long team sport, or so we thought. Yes, there was the Davis Cup, and of course the "team" concept existed at the high school and collegiate levels. You played your match, and you got a point if you won it. It was pretty much the way individual tennis went, with a twist. In 1973, that all changed. Larry King, the husband of Billie Jean King, and Chuck Reichblum developed a new concept of the game, one in which it was actually a team sport. World Team Tennis was born.

For aesthetics, the court became a mix of colorful blocks, and men and women would now be playing as one, together on the same team, where their results were equal. Then the rules were changed to make every game important. The games would be played so that the first player with four points won. This meant that ad scoring in tennis (15-30-40 then playing until one player won by two points if a game was tied at 40) was thrown out the window. This actually made the contest flow better. Every game was worth a point to the team instead of the traditional team concept of waiting until a match was won to give a team a point. So, if one team won a set 6–4, that team was leading the match 6–4. At the end of a match, which consisted of men's and women's singles, men's and women's doubles and mixed doubles, whoever won the most games was declared the winner.

Strangely, it all made sense, but if the WTT was unable to lure the best players in the world, it would be a useless venture. No one would really care. Luckily, the league was able to bring the stars to play in its new venture. Chris Evert, Billie Jean King, Bjorn Borg and Jimmy Connors, to name a few, came on board. Elton John wrote his hit song "Philadelphia Freedom" for his friend Billie Jean King, who played on—you guessed it— the Philadelphia Freedoms (although the song wasn't released until a year later after the Freedoms left Philadelphia). Jerry Buss and Robert Kraft began their lives as sports owners here by buying into the Los Angeles Strings and the Boston Lobsters, respectively. In Pittsburgh, Reichblum, lawyer Bill Sutton and famed Steel City businessman Frank Fuhrer bought Pittsburgh's entry into the league, the Triangles. They inked eight-time major winner Ken Rosewall as a player/coach before signing Wimbledon champion Evonne Goolagong and a talented young player who turned out to be a city heartthrob, Vitas Gerulaitis. It was a talented core that went 30-14 in its first season in 1974, making it to the division finals. The next year would be even better.

Rosewall was let go, and Goolagong's coach, Vic Edwards, was hired to lead the team. Peggy Michel, a member of the Intercollegiate Tennis Hall of Fame; Mark Cox; Kim Warwick; and Rayni Fox were signed to play alongside Gerulaitis and Goolagong. The results were incredible. They went 36-8 and found themselves in the league finals against the Golden Gaters from San Francisco after defeating the Lobsters in the division finals.

It was a best-of-three series. The Triangles lost at the Cow Palace in San Francisco, 26–25, blowing a 24–20 advantage, something not possible in a Davis Cup format, which made the WTT style infinitely more exciting. They came back to the Igloo and won on their home court, 28–25, which set up a third and deciding contest.

It was a warm August evening, and even though they were playing for the title, the Triangles were overshadowed by the Pittsburgh Pirates, who were on national TV in a Monday night encounter against the Braves. It's where many Pittsburgh sports fans first heard of the Triangles' exciting win, as it was announced in the middle of the broadcast.

Things did not start off well for Pittsburgh. Betty Stove and Illana Kloss crushed Goolagong and Michel in women's doubles to start off the match, putting the Triangles behind early, 6–2. Irritated at letting her team down,

The roof is the most iconic feature of the Civic Arena. In this Cory Bonnet masterpiece, he shows what supported the roof. When it was built, it was the first retractable roof on a major sports venue in the world. While later in the life of the Arena the roof wasn't able to be opened, it had already created many wonderful moments and views at events. *Courtesy of Cory Bonnet.*

the Wimbledon champ easily defeated Stove in women's singles by the same score of 6–2 to tie the game up, 8–8.

In men's doubles Gerulaitis and Cox topped Frew McMillen and Tom Okker, 7–5. The home team went into intermission with a slight 15–13 advantage. It was at that point that the G-Man, as Gerulaitis was known by his adoring female fans, took over. He toppled Okker, 6–1, in men's singles to put Pittsburgh up, 21–14. Since San Francisco could only gain six points in mixed doubles if they won 6–0, the match was over. Pittsburgh captured the Bancroft Cup, symbolic of WTT supremacy.

After one more season, the team folded, giving way to a Cleveland-Pittsburgh amalgamation that played half of their games in each city. This lasted one season. World Team Tennis was gone from the Pittsburgh landscape for good. While it never returned, it did leave the city with one thing; a final championship raised under the unique, retractable Igloo roof.

38

ELEPHANTS, DOGS AND RATS, OH MY!

ANIMALS AT THE CIVIC ARENA

BY JACK MATHISON

Animals played an interesting role in events at the Arena. As mentioned in chapter 2, the Pittsburgh Dog Show was the second-largest show in the United States at its peak. Whenever the circus came to town, it carried quite a menagerie. During one of the Ringling Bros. circus runs, the elephants were tied out in the Exhibit Hall. They were leg-tied with chain, bolts and nuts between parallel rows of chain tied to the columns in the hall. Elephants are very intelligent and creative. We always had to turn off the automatic overhead sprinkler system, because they would play with the sprinkler heads and had previously set the fire alarm off on more than one occasion. One of them got bored overnight and managed to unbolt his leg ties, which was discovered when the trainer came in the next morning. The animal didn't leave his position between the chains, but he certainly could have gone roaming if he was inclined.

Another day when the circus was in town, one of the cat trainers had a cheetah out of the cage and was training him on the floor. The cat ran from him into the adjacent ring. The cleaning crew working in the stands saw the cat run, and they did, too. We had to get several of the workers out of the restrooms once the cat was back under control. They had hidden in the restrooms, several standing on toilets with the stall doors locked!

When a rodeo was produced at the Arena, workers were loading the bulls back into trucks at the conclusion of the event. One of the bulls came within inches of escaping out of the chute at Gate 2 and could have headed out to

Center Avenue for a tour of the town. According to the bull crew chief, they would have had to saddle up horses and done a roundup in the city streets.

The trash dumpster was located outside at Gate 5 on the north side of the building. Because it was outside the building, we would occasionally get rats inside near that entrance. The situation became untenable during one summer, so the decision was made to bring in exterminators to gas a two-foot-wide landscaped area next to the driveway, because rat tunnels had been detected there. This was going to be a bit of a spectacle, so when the gassing began, many of the crew on duty went out to watch. Once the gas began to penetrate the tunnels, hundreds of rats came running out. There was a ten-foot wall adjacent to the drive, and rats climbed the wall and ran over some of the crew members who had chosen to watch from there. When asked after this show was over, one of the exterminators who had done many of these jobs said that probably five hundred rats had been in the den; only about half of them usually make it out. They plugged the tunnel entrances to keep the smell down from the decomposition for a few weeks.

So, in the end, it wasn't always the scheduled animal shows that created the most excitement at the Igloo. The running of the rats at Gate 5 was perhaps the most memorable, at least to the people who worked there.

39

FORGOTTEN BUT...WELL...STILL FORGOTTEN

THE OTHER TEAMS AND EVENTS AT THE IGLOO
WE MAY NOT REMEMBER

BY DAVID FINOLI

I've always had what some would describe as a passion; others might call it a sickness. I love the experience of seeing whatever sport this city has to offer. There's a feel and excitement about seeing games live that you just can't replicate on TV, even when it comes to teams like these that rarely appeared on TV. That's why I made sure I took the opportunity to see these teams, as well as the one event described at the end of the chapter. It was a good thing I didn't wait to experience these teams, because all were here for only a fleeting moment.

THE PITTSBURGH STINGERS

During my latter stages of high school and in my tenure at Duquesne University, I became a huge fan of the Major Indoor Soccer League (MISL) franchise that made the Civic Arena its home, the Pittsburgh Spirit. Stan Terlecki was one of my heroes. When Spirit owner Edward J. DeBartolo, who of course also owned their Civic Arena brethren the Pittsburgh Penguins, folded the team in 1986, I was a bitter man.

Fast-forward eight years. Penguins owner Howard Baldwin was interested in building a Civic Arena sporting empire of his own. The first entity would be a return of my beloved indoor soccer to the facility. It wouldn't be another

MISL squad but one in the fledgling Continental Indoor Soccer League, the Pittsburgh Stingers. I was there at the opener against Arizona, which they won, 10–4, in front of 5,917 soccer fans.

Pittsburgh quickly forgot about the Stingers. With a cumulative record of 23-33 over two seasons and a poor average attendance of 3,091, the team and indoor soccer were gone from the Steel City for good when Baldwin closed up shop in 1995.

THE PITTSBURGH PHANTOMS

As if indoor soccer wasn't enough, Baldwin started another franchise, a team that played roller hockey. Inline hockey has become popular around the country, especially in Pittsburgh, where kids have been trying to emulate Mario Lemieux on concrete for four decades. Baldwin wanted to capitalize on the vast popularity of the Pens and Lemieux and created the Pittsburgh Phantoms.

The Phantoms, named after a Kennywood Park roller coaster, had it all: the Penguins as a support staff and Hall of Famer Bryan Trottier as well as former Pens Warren Young and Alain Lemieux on its roster. They played with an orange puck and had very cool shirts (I own one). The Arena roof was opened for a contest against Minnesota. The team finished 13-9 and won a playoff series but could draw only 3,587 fans per game. After one season, Baldwin shut it down. But hey, at least I still have the jersey.

THE PITTSBURGH BULLS AND PITTSBURGH CROSSFIRE

Lacrosse came to Pittsburgh twice, and twice the town proved it wasn't a lacrosse town. I was excited when it was announced that professional lacrosse was coming to Pittsburgh and was on hand with a crowd of 9,213 fans to see the Bulls beat New England in their first game, 14–11. That was the highlight. They had matching 5-12 records and were gone in 1993.

Seven years later, the Crossfire of the National Lacrosse League moved to the Igloo from Baltimore. Bad attendance despite a decent 6-6 season sent them packing for Washington after only one season.

One of the greatest scorers in the history of men's basketball at the University of Pittsburgh is Larry Harris. He is the third-leading scorer in school history with 1,914 points and was a pivotal part of the growth of the program, which was 6–21 in 1977 before garnering a bid to the NCAA Tournament four years later. *Courtesy of the University of Pittsburgh Athletics.*

THE PITTSBURGH XPLOSION

They were the team that no one wanted, moving from the Civic Arena to the Petersen Events Center before closing the doors after the 2008 season. Playing two years in the new version of the ABA, the first year under the name the Pit Bulls and two in the Continental Basketball Association, the Xplosion had some success on the hardwood, losing twice in the league semifinals. Their roster at times included Pitt stars such as Carl Krauser and Antonio Graves, but their lasting moment in time was when their coach, Tom Washington, had a myocardial infraction during the first game in franchise history and tragically died.

In the long run, fans weren't interested in attending games with a team that couldn't properly spell its nickname. The franchise went under after four years.

THE 1983 UNITED STATES FIGURE SKATING CHAMPIONSHIP

Truth be told, of everything on this list, this was probably the one event I wasn't interested in going to. But I went, buying tickets as a Christmas present for the girl I was dating at Duquesne at the time with the full expectation that she would take her friends to see the event. Unfortunately, no one else wanted to go see figure skating, so I was forced to attend the events with her.

She patiently tried to explain the sport, but my takeaway was that, while it was much better than I had expected, the judging was inconsistent, and my complaints seemed to fall on the deaf ears on the skating crowd at the Arena. Still, I developed a crush on Rosalynn Summers, who won the ladies' title, and saw an exciting matchup between Scott Hamilton and Brian Boitano for the men's championship, won by Hamilton.

In the end, did I fall in love with the sport? Probably not, especially ice dancing—I had to wonder what the purpose was. But in the long run, I enjoyed it more than I thought I would and can proudly include it in my list of things I saw at the Igloo.

BIBLIOGRAPHY

Newspapers

Beaver County (PA) Times
Pittsburgh Post-Gazette
Pittsburgh Press

Standard Observer (Irwin, PA)
Tribune Review (Pittsburgh, PA)
Youngstown (OH) Vindicator

Magazines

Blue Ribbon College Basketball Yearbook
NCAA Football Guide
The Sporting News

Sport Magazine
Sports Illustrated

Websites

Baseball-reference.com
Basketball-reference.com
Bleacherreport.com
Corybonnet.com
ESPN.com
Goduquesne.com

Hockeydb.com
Hockey-reference.com
MLB.com
NBA.com
NFL.com
NHL.com

Pittsburghpanthers.com
Pittsburghpenguins.com
Pittsburghpirates.com
Pittsburghsteelers.com

SABR.org
Theathletic.com
Triblive.com

Media Guides

Pittsburgh Penguins
Pittsburgh Pirates
Pittsburgh Steelers

University of Pittsburgh basketball
University of Pittsburgh football
Duquesne University basketball

Books

Finoli, David. *Classic Pens*. 2nd ed Kent, Ohio: Kent State University Press., 2017.
———. *When Pitt Ruled the Gridiron*. Jefferson, NC: McFarland & Company Inc., 2014.
Finoli, David, and Bill Ranier. *The Pittsburgh Pirates Encyclopedia*. 2nd ed. N.p.: Sports Publishing Inc., 2015.
Finoli, David, and Chris Fletcher. *Steel City Gridirons*. Pittsburgh, PA: Towers Maguire Publishing, 2006.
James, Bill. *The New Bill James Historical Baseball Abstract*. New York: Free Press, 2001.

ABOUT THE AUTHORS

Growing up in Greensburg, Pennsylvania, DAVID FINOLI is a passionate fan of western Pennsylvania sports, which has been the subject of most of the books he has produced. A graduate of the Duquesne University School of Journalism, where he is featured on the "Wall of Fame" in Duquesne's Journalism and Multimedia Department, Finoli has penned thirty-three books that have highlighted the stories of the great franchises in this area, such as the Pirates, Penguins, Steelers, Duquesne basketball and Pitt football, to name a few. His latest book, *Pittsburgh's Greatest Players*, not only ranks the top fifty players in western Pennsylvania history but also includes a list of every Hall of Fame athlete who represented the area. Winner of the 2018 *Pittsburgh Magazine*'s Best of the 'Burgh local author award, Finoli lives in Monroeville, Pennsylvania, with his wife, Vivian. He also has three children, Tony, Cara, Matt; his daughter-in-law Chynna; and three grandchildren, River, Emmy and Ellie.

TOM ROONEY had three stretches of duty at the Civic Arena. As an usher while matriculating across the way at Duquesne University, he worked at least one hundred events a year for four years (1969–73), a great way to see his beloved Penguins and actually get paid for it. For a decade (1981–90), he worked for the DeBartolo-owned Civic Arena Corporation, running and promoting events and marketing teams like the Pens, soccer Spirit and indoor football Gladiators. Then, he spent four more years (1999–2003) working for Mario Lemieux as president of the Pens. Under the dome was his home away from home.

CHRIS FLETCHER, based in Forest Hills, Pennsylvania, is a writer, marketer, fundraiser and all-around swell guy. He was the former publisher and editor of *Pittsburgh Magazine*; not only did Chris win ten Golden Quill Awards while working at the magazine, but also under his direction the magazine was awarded the prestigious White Award as the country's top city magazine in 1995 from the City and Regional Magazine Association. Fletcher also teamed up with David Finoli to author two other sports books, *Steel City Gridirons* and *The Steel City 500*. A 1984 graduate of Duquesne University's journalism program, Chris still dreams of catching one more contest in the old Civic Arena (provided it wouldn't be in one of the obstructed-view seats).

JOSH TAYLOR is a sports anchor and reporter with KDKA-TV in Pittsburgh, as well as a weekend sports talk radio host at 93.7 FM, "The Fan." A native of Pittsburgh, Josh was raised in the Hill District section of the city and is a graduate of Schenley High School and Duquesne University. He has won a Telly Award and two Associated Press awards for his work as a journalist and was honored as one of the *New Pittsburgh Courier*'s "Men of Excellence" in 2017. He is also featured on the "Wall of Fame" in Duquesne's Journalism and Multimedia Department.

ROBERT EDWARD HEALY III, a Pittsburgh native, is a professor in the media department at Duquesne University and the cofounder of Duquesne's Sports Information and Media department. Prior to teaching, Robert worked three-year stints as a sports information director and as a news reporter, respectively. He and his wife, Nicole, live in Pittsburgh's South Hills area with their daughters, Rhiannon and Josephine.

PAUL ALEXANDER began his career in sports broadcasting while attending Churchill High School. He picked the perfect year to be the sports guy on the wildly popular *Before the Bell* show that went over the school's PA system. You should recall that 1979 christened Pittsburgh as the City of Champions, with the Pirates winning the World Series and the Steelers capturing their fourth Lombardi Trophy in a six-year span.

Next up was Penn State, where Paul procured a spot on the staff of the school's daily paper. He realized after a week in New Orleans covering the Nittany Lions' first NCAA National Championship that he simply had to do this as long as he could. That electrifying win over Herschel Walker and Georgia in the 1982 Sugar Bowl was addicting. Paul didn't miss covering a Penn State football game until he finally made it home to Pittsburgh in 1998, when he was named the morning anchor at KDKA-TV.

That started a wild ride through the 'Burgh's various media outlets. He had his own show on KDKA radio and was the Steelers' beat reporter at FSN and pre- and postgame host for the Pirates and Penguins on ROOT Sports and AT&T Sportsnet. He also managed to be the original host on the FAN morning show on 93.7 FM.

Paul is married and has five kids, a granddaughter and his dog, Murphy.

JOHN W. FRANKO is a 1985 graduate of Duquesne University with a BA in journalism and a master's in religious education. While at Duquesne, he was a proud member of Sigma Tau Gamma fraternity. He has been a staff member of the *Pittsburgh Catholic* newspaper since 1990 and has been recognized nationally for his work. John is a loyal supporter of the Duquesne University women's basketball team, where his sister Melissa is director of basketball operations. Go Dukes! John is a longtime resident of Pittsburgh's North Hills. He has been an ardent supporter of Pittsburgh sports teams for nearly fifty years and has many memorable moments, among them the 2013 Pirates' Wild Card game and Troy Polamalu's interception against the Ravens in the AFC championship game. His favorite Pirate was Richie "Hepner" (that's how he spelled it on his glove!).

GARY KINN is a graduate of the Duquesne University journalism program, which he completed concurrently with David Finoli and Chris Fletcher. He has worked in commercial banking and real estate finance in the Philadelphia area since 1983. He has religiously followed professional baseball, hockey and boxing since 1970 and is an avid historian of all three sports. He has also attended more than one hundred live championship boxing cards in the United States, including in New York City, Atlantic City and Las Vegas. He lives in New Jersey and still believes that stolen bases are as exciting and important as home runs and strikeouts, that ties in hockey are an acceptable outcome and that there is only world champion in boxing's eight weight-class divisions.

LANCE JONES is a thirty-plus-year veteran of the music industry. Starting on the path after college in 1976 by clerking in an indie record store, he then took a position with Warner-Elektra-Atlantic Distributing Corporation as the company's southwestern Pennsylvania field merchandiser beginning in 1978. In 1980, Jones joined National Record Mart as the chain's in-store merchandiser and rose to the director of advertising position in 1982. Three years later, he signed on as the new director of booking for the Pittsburgh Civic Arena and, in 1991, left indoors for outdoors, landing employment at Star Lake Amphitheater (now Key Bank Pavilion) as director of marketing. In 1995, Jones ascended to general manager of Star Lake, a position he held until he left the company for nonprofit endeavors in early 2008. Jones joined local PBS affiliate and community broadcaster WQED Multimedia in September 2009.

Pittsburgh native FRANK GARLAND is a longtime journalist, author and college professor with a lifelong passion for baseball. He worked for more than thirty years at several northern California newspapers and since 2005 has been teaching at Gannon University in Erie, Pennsylvania. His biography of Willie Stargell, *Willie Stargell: A Life in Baseball*, was published in 2013 by McFarland & Company, and a biography of Pirates Hall of Famer Arky Vaughan, titled *Arky: The Baseball Life of Joseph Floyd "Arky" Vaughan*, was published by McFarland in August 2020..

DOUGLAS CAVANAUGH is a freelance writer living in Los Angeles. His most recent projects include collaborating on the book *Rooney-McGinley Boxing Club* with Art Rooney Jr., as well as his own book, *Pittsburgh Boxing: A Pictorial History*. He currently runs a popular Pittsburgh boxing history page on Facebook.

JACK MATHISON has worked in public assembly facilities and organizations his entire professional life. He holds a master's in sports administration from Ohio University. He served at the Civic Arena from August 1973 to

December 1984 as sales manager, assistant executive director and then vice president of Arena Operations. He also worked at the Fort Lauderdale Stadiums and Special Facilities and with the Hollywood Florida Parks and Recreation Department. He also worked at the Equestrian Center for the 1996 Atlanta Olympics. In his semi-retirement years, he was a part-time sales representative for Foreverlawn, a synthetic turf company. He is presently retired and lives in Hobe Sound, Florida.

Having said to himself that he would be the next "Woodward and Bernstein combined" while studying investigative journalism in college, JOHN WDOWIAK's professional path took a hard right turn after graduating from Duquesne University, where he found time to go to class between playing intramural hockey and working on the *Duquesne Duke* student newspaper. After bouncing around covering high school, college and professional sports for the *Daily Messenger* in Homestead, the *South Hills Record* and then the *Pittsburgh Press*, John switched to a career in PR/marketing in 1985 but never forgot his roots. Since 1995, John has been fortunate to be the marketing director for Coldwell Banker Real Estate in Pittsburgh. He has a passion for all sports, didn't miss a Steeler home game for fifteen consecutive seasons and became a hockey junkie at age eleven, when he used to imagine himself as Tony Esposito in goal, except that he had trouble fitting the plastic goalie mask over his glasses. Today, John watches probably more hockey than he should, attends roughly fifteen to twenty Penguin games a year and lives with his wife, Corinne, in Bethel Park. He can't spend enough time with his three grown children, Sarah (and her husband, Phill), Kelly and Ethan. When he's not working or watching a game, John enjoys long trail walks with his dog, Jack, and discovering new vinyl at independent record stores.

RICHARD BOYER grew up in the South Hills of Pittsburgh an avid sports and concert fan. He attended his first hockey game at the Igloo in 1969 and closed it out at the last concert. In between, as a Penguin season ticket holder, he experienced some of the greatest moments in Pittsburgh sports history. After graduating from Duquesne University in 1980, he spent his career in the insurance industry as an underwriter, account executive and now president of Exchange Underwriters, an independent insurance agency located in Washington, Pennsylvania. He is a director and senior vice-president of Community Bank and a chartered property and casualty underwriter, as well as a director with a minority ownership in Stoney's Brewing Company. Rich has always had a passion for writing and is grateful for the chance that Dave Finoli has given him in this book. Rich currently resides in the South Hills with his wife, Wendy, and two dogs, Sarah and Sallie. He has four children, Jason, Jessica, Joshua and Jennifer.